TRANSFORMED

THE GIFT AND CHALLENGE
OF THE EUCHARIST

A Catholic Guide for Small Groups

Published by The Evangelical Catholic
6602 Normandy Lane FL 2
Madison, WI 53719
www.evangelicalcatholic.org

27 26 25 24 23 1 2 3 4 5 6

Nihil obstat: Mr. Timothy Cavanaugh
                  Censor Deputatus
                  September 25, 2023

Imprimatur: + James Robert Bartylla
                  Vicar General of the Diocese of Madison
                  September 24, 2023

ISBN: 979-8-9891366-2-9
eISBN: 979-8-9891366-3-6

Cover design by Andrea Jackson
Book design by Darlene Swanson • www.van-garde.com

Made and printed in the United States of America.

Contents

Introduction

Catholics believe an astonishing thing: that the body, blood, soul, and divinity of Christ are available to us under the appearances of bread and wine offered at every Mass.[1] This gift of himself that Jesus supplies us—the Eucharist—stands at the very center of the Catholic faith, as "the source and summit of the Christian life."[2]

What effect does this indescribable gift have on us? One word captures it well: *transformation*. As the substance of bread and wine are truly *transformed* into the Body and Blood of Jesus, we who receive this heavenly meal with open hearts are continually *transformed* into people who love like Jesus—and loving like Jesus *transforms* the world.

---

1   Cf. *Catechism of the Catholic Church, 2nd ed.* (Washington, D.C.: United States Conference of Catholic Bishops, 2016), 1374.

2   *Catechism of the Catholic Church*, 1324, cf. *Lumen gentium*, 11.

The force at the center of all this transforming power, which acts "like nuclear fission at the very heart of being"[3] is the Paschal Mystery: the Death and the Resurrection of Jesus Christ, the Word made flesh.

> By making the bread into his Body and the wine into his Blood, [Jesus] anticipates his death, he accepts it in his heart, and he transforms it into an action of love... This is the substantial transformation which was accomplished at the Last Supper and was destined to set in motion a series of transformations leading ultimately to the transformation of the world when God will be all in all (cf. 1 Cor 15:28).[4]

This book is a guide for communal exploration and discussion around this "series of transformations" that the Paschal Mystery, made present to us in the Eucharist, has set in motion. It is a transformation

- from death to life (Session 1);

- from bread to Body (Session 2);

---

3   Benedict XVI, "Homily at Mass for the Twentieth World Youth Day, August 21, 2005" in *Pope Benedict XVI: The Eucharist* (Washington, D.C.: USCCB Publishing, 2009), 3.
4   *Ibid.*

- from heaven to earth (Session 3);

- from time to eternity (Session 4);

- from human to divine (Session 5); and

- from the table to the world (Session 6).

Each of these transformations comes to us as both a gift and challenge.

The intended audience for this discussion guide is people of faith who want to reflect on Scripture and Catholic teaching surrounding the Eucharist. Many worthy books and courses teach the finer theological points of the mystery of the Eucharist. This guide, instead, aims to draw groups into prayerful reflection and discussion on this mystery. Through a thoughtful arrangement of biblical themes, traditional prayers, and pointed questions, you are invited to deepen your experience of Mass and clarify the implications of Eucharistic worship for your daily life in the world. For those desiring a systematic presentation of Church teaching on the Eucharist, see our list of recommended readings at the end of the next section.

Our hope is that, as you gather in community to reflect on the sacred mystery of the Eucharist, your hearts will burn with new love and ardor for Christ and for the world he came to save.

How to Use this Book

While an individual may benefit from reading and reflecting on this book alone, we recommend you use it in pairs or in small groups of up to roughly ten people. The community of faith and the collective experiences, comments, and questions of those who gather to reflect and pray together often proves to be the most valuable ingredient in the spiritual exploration of a topic such as this. Of course, we know exactly why this would be the case, for our Lord himself has promised: "Where two or three are gathered in my name, I am there among them" (Matthew 18:20).

Weekly Sessions

The six weekly session materials contain the core content of this guide. Here you will find opening and closing prayers, often drawing in part upon prayers from the Mass or the Eucharistic hymns and prayers of St. Thomas Aquinas. There is an opening discussion, followed by two selections from Scripture and

Church Tradition. This section makes up the bulk of your conversation. Discussion questions are provided throughout. The "Final Thoughts" subsection provides a short essay to read aloud which recaps themes from the session and points participants to three suggested prompts for further prayer, reading, and action throughout the coming week. They can find further instructions and helpful prompts for those actions in the subsection "Encountering Christ This Week."

Each session is intended for a ninety-minute small group format. While we strongly recommend ninety-minute sessions, you may wish to adjust these slightly according to your own group's size, style, and desired length. For example, if you have just three people that meet before work or school, you could theoretically keep each session to sixty or seventy-five minutes. Whatever you choose, be sure to start and end on time to honor each person's time and other commitments. See page 135 for a session-by-session timing guide.

It is best if every participant has a copy of the book, allowing them to fully participate in the group sessions and the at-home suggestions. When the group is gathered, each person can read aloud at times and look back over the readings or questions as they ponder their thoughts and contribute to the conversation.

Appendices

Helpful appendices for both participants and facilitators supplement the weekly materials. Appendices A through E are for everyone, and Appendix F is for group facilitators.

Prior to your first meeting, please read Appendix A, "Small Group Discussion Guidelines." These guidelines will help every person in the group set a respectful tone that creates the space for encountering Christ together. They will help everyone understand the goal of seeking a Spirit-led discussion and give you helpful tidbits for being a supportive and involved member of the group.

Appendix B is a primer on prayer and Scripture meditation to deepen your relationship with God. In it you will find step-by-step guides for praying in your own words and reflecting prayerfully on Scripture in your personal prayer times. Reading this appendix can help you go deeper with the key Scripture passages listed in the "Encountering Christ This Week" section of each weekly discussion guide.

Appendix C contains a concise guide to the Sacrament of Reconciliation. Commonly known as "confession," the Sacrament of Reconciliation bridges the distance between us and God (and the community of faith) that can be caused by a variety of reasons, including unrepented sin. If you want to grow closer to Jesus and experience great peace, as well as get the most out of the Eucharist, the Sacrament of Reconciliation is an indispensable gift. This appendix leads you through the steps of preparing for and going to confession in order to lessen any anxiety you might feel.

Appendices D and E contain short essays that fill in potential gaps in your understanding of the biblical background (Appendix D) or the broader principles of Catholic theology (Appendix E) behind some of the texts discussed in the weekly sessions. These are presented as suggested readings in the contents of sessions 1 and 2 respectively.

Finally, Appendix F is for group facilitators. It contains guidance and best practices for facilitating a Spirit-filled discussion in a way that honors each member and encourages participation as each feels comfortable.

For Further Study on the Eucharist

As stated above, this resource presumes a basic acceptance of Catholic teaching on the Eucharist. If you would like to further explore this teaching, consider some or all of the following sources.

- *Catechism of the Catholic Church,* sections 1322-1419

- *Compendium on the Eucharist,* United States Conference of Catholic Bishops, 2009

- *Real Presence: What Does it Mean and Why Does it Matter?* Timothy P. O'Malley, Ave Maria Press, 2021

- *Bored Again Catholic: How the Mass Could Save Your Life* Timothy P. O'Malley, Our Sunday Visitor, 2017

- *Eucharist,* Bishop Robert Barron, Word on Fire, 2021

- *God Is Near Us: The Eucharist, The Heart of Life,* Joseph Cardinal Ratzinger (Pope Benedict XVI), 2003

- *The Lamb's Supper: The Mass as Heaven on Earth,* Scott Hahn, Doubleday, 1999

Eucharistic Prayers of St. Thomas Aquinas

Special thanks to Sophia Institute Press for giving permission to use the prayers of St. Thomas Aquinas from *The Aquinas Prayer Book: The Prayers and Hymns of St. Thomas Aquinas*, translated and edited by Robert Anderson and Johann Moser. This edition of St. Thomas' prayers is available for purchase at sophiainstitute.com/product/the-aquinas-prayer-book/

Session 1:
From Death to Life

*Just as Christ was raised from the
dead by the glory of the Father, so we too
might walk in newness of life.*
– Romans 6:4

Group Introductions

- If this is a new small group, take some time to get to know each other a bit. Each person can share a little about themself and why they were interested in joining this group.

- If it's a returning small group but it has been a while since you met, take a few minutes for each person to share what they've been up to lately.

- If you're an established small group already acquainted with one another, feel free to socialize briefly and then jump into the session.

Opening Prayer

Invite someone to read the following introduction and prayer aloud.

In most of the opening prayers throughout this discussion guide, we'll read a traditional Eucharistic prayer or hymn as part of the opening prayer. Allow these hymns and prayers to teach or remind you of what we believe the Eucharist to be, and to set a tone of wonder and gratitude in the forthcoming discussions.

In the name of the Father, and of the Son, and of the Holy Spirit. Amen.

Thank you, Lord, for the opportunity to gather and discuss your Word. Please use our readings and discussion today, including the prayer of St. Thomas Aquinas we now read, to heighten our anticipation for the next time we are able to receive your Body and Blood in the Eucharist. Help us prepare to come to you with humble, reverent, and contrite hearts.

Let us pray:

> *God, Who left for us*
> *a memorial of Your Passion*
> *in this miraculous sacrament,*
>
> *Grant, we implore You,*
> *that we may venerate*
> *the holy mystery of Your Body and Blood,*
> *so that we may ever experience in ourselves*
> *the fruitfulness of Your redemption.*
>
> *You Who live and reign, world without end.*[1]

Amen.

---

1   Thomas Aquinas, "To the Most Holy Sacrament," in *The Aquinas Prayer Book: The Prayers and Hymns of St. Thomas Aquinas,* translated and edited by Robert Anderson and Johann Moser (Manchester, NH: Sophia Institute Press, 2000), 61, 63.

Opening Discussion

Answer some or all of the following questions.

1. What are you hoping for as you begin this small group experience?

2. What about the Eucharist or the Mass appeals most to you?

3. What about the Eucharist or the Mass remains mysterious, strange, or difficult for you?

Scripture and Tradition

Invite two or three people to read the introductory paragraph and Scripture passage aloud.

Early in the Mass, the priest invites us "to prepare ourselves to celebrate the *sacred mysteries.*" "Sacred mysteries" is an apt term for the Mass and the Eucharist. They are at once so holy, special, and profound (sacred) that our minds can never *fully* comprehend all the richness they contain (mystery).

The Eucharist, according to Catholic experience and teaching, is not merely a symbol reminding us of Jesus. The reservoirs of symbolism and memory are far too shallow to contain the depths of Jesus' words and actions surrounding this sacred meal. Centuries of canonized Saints and everyday believers bear witness to the shocking reality that, "in the most blessed sacrament of the Eucharist the body and blood, together with the soul and divinity, of our Lord Jesus Christ and, therefore, *the whole Christ is truly, really, and substantially* contained."[2]

This book guides you to reflect on and discuss themes, prayers, and Scripture passages that inform our practice and belief in the Eucharist as "the source and summit of the Christian life."[3] Your reflections will encompass themes drawn from the Old and New Testaments, wisdom from Church Tradition, and from various prayers and hymns of the Church. Just as importantly, you will be prompted to share your own thoughts, questions, and experiences surrounding these "sacred mysteries."

If there is one theme we hope becomes increasingly clear throughout these discussions, it is found on the cover: *transformation*. The substance of bread and wine are truly *transformed* into Jesus' Body and Blood. We who receive this heavenly meal with open

---

2   *Catechism of the Catholic Church*, 1374, quoting Paul VI in *Mysterium fidei*, 39.
3   *Catechism of the Catholic Church*, 1324, cf. *Lumen gentium*, 11.

hearts are continually *transformed* into people who love like Jesus. And loving like Jesus *transforms* the world.

In today's conversation, consider how Jesus' sacrifice of his Body and Blood opened up a new path away from sin and death and into freedom and life.

Luke 22:14-20

[14] When the hour came, he took his place at the table, and the apostles with him. [15] He said to them, "I have eagerly desired to eat this Passover with you before I suffer; [16] for I tell you, I will not eat it until it is fulfilled in the kingdom of God." [17] Then he took a cup, and after giving thanks he said, "Take this and divide it among yourselves; [18] for I tell you that from now on I will not drink of the fruit of the vine until the kingdom of God comes." [19] Then he took a loaf of bread, and when he had given thanks, he broke it and gave it to them, saying, "This is my body, which is given for you. Do this in remembrance of me." [20] And he did the same with the cup after

supper, saying, "This cup that is poured out for you is the new covenant in my blood."

Discuss

1. If you knew you were going to die in a few days, what are some things you would do with the time you had remaining?

2. How does thinking about this affect how you read these words of Jesus, who knew his death was imminent?

3. What event in Israel's history does the Jewish feast of Passover celebrate and memorialize?

4. How do Jesus' words at the Last Supper, a Passover meal on the eve of his death, give new meaning to the ultimate "Passover" of God's people from slavery to sin and death into freedom and life?[4]

5. How might this understanding of the historical context of Passover and the Eucharist affect your experience of Mass?

---

4   For more on this topic, see Appendix D: Lamb of God.

Invite someone to read the following aloud.

Pope Benedict XVI

By making the bread into his Body and the wine into his Blood, [Jesus] anticipates his death, he accepts it in his heart, and he transforms it into an action of love. What on the outside is simply brutal violence—the Crucifixion—from within becomes an act of total self-giving love. This is the substantial transformation which was accomplished at the Last Supper and was destined to set in motion a series of transformations leading ultimately to the transformation of the world when God will be all in all (cf. 1 Cor 15:28). In their hearts, people always and everywhere have somehow expected a change, a transformation of the world. Here now is the central act of transformation that alone can truly renew the world: violence is transformed into love, and death into life. Since this act transmutes death into love, death as such is already conquered from within, the Resurrection is already present in it.

Death is, so to speak, mortally wounded, so that it can no longer have the last word. To use an image well known to us today, this is like inducing nuclear fission in the very heart of being—the victory of love over hatred, the victory of love over death. Only this intimate explosion of good conquering evil can then trigger off the series of transformations that little by little will change the world. All other changes remain superficial and cannot save. For this reason we speak of redemption: what had to happen at the most intimate level has indeed happened, and we can enter into its dynamic. Jesus can distribute his Body, because he truly gives himself.[5]

Discuss

1. What words or phrases stand out to you from this quote by Pope Benedict? How do you understand what he's saying?

---

5   Benedict XVI, "Homily at Mass for the Twentieth World Youth Day, August 21, 2005," in *Pope Benedict XVI: The Eucharist* (Washington, D.C.: USCCB Publishing, 2009), 3.

2. What connections do you see between the Last Supper and Jesus' death?

3. What effects do Jesus' Death and Resurrection have on the world?

4. Pope Benedict says that death is "mortally wounded" and "can no longer have the last word." How do you understand this in a world that still experiences death and the effects of sin?

5. In what ways have you experienced (or do you want to experience) the transformation that Jesus offers in the gift of himself?

6. How do you think participating in the celebration of Mass can help you enter more fully into the dynamic of redemption described here?

Final Thoughts

Invite one or two people to read aloud.

Prior to Jesus, the transformational event in the lives of the Israelites was when God freed them from slavery to the Egyptians. But despite how miraculous and majestic God's rescue was—an event they saw before their eyes—the people quickly forgot what God had done for them and turned to idols, to complaining, and to self-reliance.

Jesus gives us a way to do more than remember the miraculous and majestic rescue he waged for us through his death and resurrection. In the Eucharist we *experience* these acts of redemption as we receive Christ's Body and Blood. What he said to the disciples rings out through all time and space, as he continues to say to us: "This is my body, which is given for you" (Luke 22:19). In the Eucharist, he draws us into the transformational events of the Cross and Resurrection, offering us newness of life and freedom from sin.[6]

Before the Last Supper, Jesus sent his disciples ahead of him to make preparations for the Passover meal (Luke 22:7-13). We, too, must prepare to receive him, and Jesus gives us everything we need to do so. He can transform our sins and shame into occasions of love, mercy, and forgiveness. He can take our fears and jealousies and create in us a humble reliance on

---

6   "The Eucharist is the heart and the summit of the Church's life, for in it Christ associates his Church and all her members with his sacrifice of praise and thanksgiving offered once for all on the cross to his Father; by this sacrifice he pours out the graces of salvation on his Body which is the Church" (*Catechism of the Catholic Church*, 1407).

his grace. He can take our mustard seed of faith and give us everlasting life.

This week, say yes to the transformation Jesus offers by making special preparations to celebrate the Eucharist with a free and receptive heart by receiving the Sacrament of Reconciliation, praying with key Scriptures, and taking time to pray before receiving the Eucharist.

Bookmark the "Encounter Christ This Week" section on page 14 for help and inspiration for applying today's discussion in your life.

Closing Prayer

Invite someone to lead the group in prayer. Begin by reading the following introduction aloud.

In most of the closing prayers throughout this discussion guide, you'll find a Prayer After Communion from the Mass. The Roman Missal has different prayers after communion for every week of the liturgical year, and they are all concise, beautiful, power-packed prayers. In one sense, these prayers are out of place here, because you are not at Mass and did not just receive the Eucharist. Yet, these prayers remind us to reflect on the gifts we are privileged to receive at Mass. May they lead your hearts to long even more for Eucharistic union with Jesus.

In the name of the Father, and of the Son, and of the Holy Spirit. Amen.

Lord Jesus, who in laying down your life for us won the victory of love over hatred and death, thank you for the gift of your divine self. We need you and the victory of love you set forth in our world. Help us not only to remember but also to enter into the redemption you have won for us. Give us a greater desire to turn from all that is not of you and place you more firmly at the center of our lives.

(Add your own prayers and invite others to pray as well. Close with the following prayer from the Mass.)

Let us pray:

> *We have consumed, O Lord, this divine Sacrament, the perpetual memorial of the Passion of your Son; grant, we pray, that this gift, which he himself gave us with*

*love beyond all telling, may profit us for
salvation.*

Through Christ our Lord.[7]

Amen.

Encounter Christ This Week

*Refer to the following pages throughout the week
to incorporate this week's discussion into your life.*

Receive the Sacrament of Reconciliation (confession). Jesus taught his followers at the Sermon on the Mount: "when you are offering your gift at the altar, if you remember that your brother or sister has something against you, leave your gift there before the altar and go; first be reconciled to your brother or sister, and then come and offer your gift" (Matthew 5:23-24). Our personal sins deteriorate the communion both with Christ and with the community of the Church that the Eucharist is meant to celebrate. Regularly receiving the Sacrament of Reconciliation repairs and deepens that communion. If it has been

---

7   "Prayer After Communion, 17th Sunday in Ordinary Time," *The Roman Missal*, 3rd ed. (New Jersey: Catholic Book Publishing Corp., 2011), 331.

over a year since you've been to confession or you are aware of any sins you want to confess, seek out this healing sacrament in preparation for the Eucharist. See Appendix C on page 111 for an examination of conscience and a guide to receiving the Sacrament of Reconciliation.

Pray with key Scriptures about the transformed life Jesus offers. Pray with the following passages and journal about the questions below.

- **Galatians 5:13-26**

    » What has Jesus' death and resurrection freed you *from*? What has he freed you *for*?

    » In what areas do you still feel "enslaved" to sin, fear, sickness or other forms of death? Ask Jesus for the graces and help you need to live in greater freedom.

    » Do you know someone who radiates the fruit of the Spirit? How do they show you what it means to live in freedom?

- **1 John 4:7-21**

    » How have you received the love of Jesus in your life?

» In what ways does claiming your identity as someone beloved by God free you from fear or empower you to resist sin?

» Is there a relationship or situation in your life that needs repair? What prayer or action is Jesus' love calling you to in this situation?

Pray before receiving the Eucharist. If possible, arrive at Mass five or ten minutes before it begins to give your mind, body, and spirit a moment to settle in and be receptive to the graces God has in mind for you. Bring and pray the prayer of St. Thomas Aquinas that you read for today's opening prayer. Ask along with St. Thomas that you experience the fruitfulness of the redemption Christ has won for us. You can also pray as you approach the altar to receive the Eucharist. In that brief moment, ask God to make you fully receptive to his gifts or pray a Hail Mary, asking to have a heart like Mary's to receive Jesus fruitfully.

Session 2:
From Bread to Body

The bread that I will give is
my flesh for the life of the world.
– John 6:51 (NABRE)

Opening Prayer

Invite someone to read the opening prayer.

In the name of the Father, and of the Son, and of the Holy Spirit. Amen.

Good and everlasting God, it is truly you who we long for: the fulfillment of our desires, the answer to our prayers. Strengthen and sustain us in your goodness, O God. Let the vanities and deceptions of this world lose their sweetness for us. You alone satisfy, O Lord. Refine our tastes so that we desire more of you.

Let us pray:

> *O God, you are my God, I seek you,*
>> *my soul thirsts for you;*
> *my flesh faints for you,*
>> *as in a dry and weary land where there is no water.*
> *So I have looked upon you in the sanctuary,*
>> *beholding your power and glory.*
> *Because your steadfast love is better than life,*
>> *my lips will praise you.*
> *So I will bless you as long as I live;*
>> *I will lift up my hands and call on your name.*

My soul is satisfied as with a rich feast,
    and my mouth praises you with joyful lips.[1]

Amen.

Opening Discussion

Answer some or all the following questions.

1. Share a high and a low from the past week.

2. What spoke to you from your prayer this week?

3. What role does eating together play in your family or at family reunions and special occasions?

Scripture & Tradition

Invite two or three people to read the introductory paragraph and Scripture passage aloud.

Hunger is a pervasive theme in the Bible. After God, through Moses, freed the Israelites from slavery in Egypt, the people complained of not having food and water in the desert, and God provided for all

---

1   Psalm 63:1-5

their needs. He brought manna (bread), quail, and even water flowing from a rock. Physical hunger is also a symbol of a deeper spiritual hunger all humans share: the longing for meaning, purpose, identity, community, love. In short, we hunger for God, in whose image and likeness we are made. The psalm in the opening prayer expresses both the human longing for God as well as the experience of being deeply satisfied by God's love, protection, and blessings. Reflect today on these themes of hunger and God's provision as you read from the Bread of Life discourse in St. John's Gospel and a reflection from the *Catechism* on physical and spiritual hunger.

Selections from John 6

[30] So they said to him, "What sign are you going to give us then, so that we may see it and believe you? What work are you performing? [31] Our ancestors ate the manna in the wilderness; as it is written, 'He gave them bread from heaven to eat.'" [32] Then Jesus said to them, "Very truly, I tell you, it was not Moses who gave you the bread from heaven, but it is my Father who gives

you the true bread from heaven. [33] For the bread of God is that which comes down from heaven and gives life to the world." [34] They said to him, "Sir, give us this bread always."

[35] Jesus said to them, "I am the bread of life. Whoever comes to me will never be hungry, and whoever believes in me will never be thirsty. […]

[48] I am the bread of life. [49] Your ancestors ate the manna in the wilderness, and they died. [50] This is the bread that comes down from heaven, so that one may eat of it and not die. [51] I am the living bread that came down from heaven. Whoever eats of this bread will live forever; and the bread that I will give for the life of the world is my flesh."

[52] The Jews then disputed among themselves, saying, "How can this man give us his flesh to eat?" [53] So Jesus said to them, "Very truly, I tell you, unless you eat the flesh of the Son of Man and drink his blood, you have no life

in you. [54] Those who eat my flesh and drink my blood have eternal life, and I will raise them up on the last day; [55] for my flesh is true food and my blood is true drink. [56] Those who eat my flesh and drink my blood abide in me, and I in them. [57] Just as the living Father sent me, and I live because of the Father, so whoever eats me will live because of me. [58] This is the bread that came down from heaven, not like that which your ancestors ate, and they died. But the one who eats this bread will live forever." [...]

[66] As a result of this, many [of] his disciples returned to their former way of life and no longer accompanied him. [67] Jesus then said to the Twelve, "Do you also want to leave?" [68] Simon Peter answered him, "Master, to whom shall we go? You have the words of eternal life. [69] We have come to believe and are convinced that you are the Holy One of God."

Discuss

1. Jesus says that he gives his flesh "for the life of the world." What do you think Jesus

means by "life" here? What other verses help you understand what he is saying?

2. "I am the bread of life. Whoever comes to me will never be hungry, and whoever believes in me will never be thirsty." How do you make sense of these words, given that we all still experience both physical and spiritual hunger/thirst?

3. What role do Mass and the Eucharist play for you in staying connected to the life Jesus came to give?

4. Understandably, the people listening to Jesus in this passage struggle to make sense of what he is saying. Do you ever find it difficult to believe in the Real Presence of Jesus in the Eucharist?

5. How is Peter the same as the disciples who returned to their former way of life? How is he different?

6. How can you apply Peter's response in your own life of discipleship?

Invite someone to read the following aloud.

Catechism of the Catholic Church

1391 Holy Communion augments our union with Christ. The principal fruit of receiving the Eucharist in Holy Communion is an intimate union with Christ Jesus. Indeed, the Lord said: "He who eats my flesh and drinks my blood abides in me, and I in him."[226] Life in Christ has its foundation in the Eucharistic banquet: "As the living Father sent me, and I live because of the Father, so he who eats me will live because of me."[227]

On the feasts of the Lord, when the faithful receive the Body of the Son, they proclaim to one another the Good News that the first fruits of life have been given, as when the angel said to Mary Magdalene, "Christ is risen!" Now too are life and resurrection conferred on whoever receives Christ.[228]

1392 What material food produces in our bodily life, Holy Communion wonderfully achieves in our spiritual life. Communion with the flesh of the risen Christ, a flesh "given life and giving life through the Holy Spirit,"[229] preserves, increases, and renews the life of grace received at Baptism. This growth in Christian life needs the nourishment of Eucharistic Communion, the bread for our pilgrimage until the moment of death, when it will be given to us as viaticum.[2]

Discuss

1. Consider the connection the *Catechism* makes between material food and spiritual food. What are the results of putting "good" foods versus "junk" foods into your system? Is there a material food you needed to acquire a taste for over time?

2. What insights from your experience of material food might apply to your experience of the spiritual food of the Eucharist?

---

2   *Catechism of the Catholic Church*, 1391-1392. Footnotes from CCC:
     226 *Jn* 6:56.
     227 *Jn* 6:57.
     228 Fanqith, Syriac Office of Antioch, Vol. I, Commun., 237a-b.
     229 Presbyterorum ordinis 5.

3. How do you understand or experience what is meant by "intimate union with Christ Jesus" in paragraph 1391?

Final Thoughts

Invite one or two people to read aloud.

"Those who seek the Lord lack no good thing" (Psalm 34:10). God provides for his people—both materially and spiritually—though not always in the ways we want or understand. The Israelites, kept alive by the manna, did plenty of complaining about its less-than-thrilling taste compared to the rich foods they enjoyed while enslaved in Egypt. And when Jesus revealed the ultimate gift of Bread from heaven, which is himself, the response from his closest friends was one of mustered trust rather than of pure delight and understanding.

Whether we feel deeply moved by the beauty and truth of the Eucharist or we're left scratching our heads before such a profound mystery of faith, we can say with St. Peter, "Master, to whom shall we go? You have the words of eternal life" (John 6:68). Just as it often takes time and maturity to acquire tastes for the foods that are best for our bodies, so it can be with what is best for our souls. As we follow Christ, he transforms our desires and appetites, teaching us to "hunger and thirst for righteousness" (Matthew 5:6). By returning, again and again, to the heavenly meal of the Eucharist, we acquire the taste of heaven itself.

In the week ahead concentrate on relying more fully on the provisions of God by adding an additional daily Mass to your week if you're able, praying with key Scriptures about God feeding his people, and reading the short essay "No Life in You?" in Appendix E on page 125.

Bookmark the "Encounter Christ This Week" section on page 28 for help and inspiration for applying today's discussion in your life.

Closing Prayer

Invite someone to lead the group in prayer.

In the name of the Father, and of the Son, and of the Holy Spirit. Amen.

Lord, thank you for this time we have shared together in your name, sitting at the table of your Word. Only you know which part of our conversation is most fruitful for each of us to remember. Help us hold onto these things as we depart from here.

We lift up our own hopes and petitions to your loving care:

(Add your own prayers and invite others to pray as well. Close with the following prayer.)

> *Renewed now with heavenly bread, by which faith is nourished, hope increased, and charity strengthened, we pray, O Lord, that we may learn to hunger for Christ, the true and living Bread, and strive to live by every word which proceeds from your mouth. Through Christ our Lord.*[3]

Amen.

Encounter Christ This Week

Refer to the following pages throughout the week to incorporate this week's discussion into your life.

Go to Mass one more day than you typically do. Unless you already go to Mass seven days a week, add one daily Mass to your routine. Recall Jesus'

---

3   "Prayer After Communion, 1st Sunday of Lent," 80.

words, which precede the selection you read today: "Do not work for the food that perishes, but for the food that endures for eternal life, which the Son of Man will give you" (John 6:27). Consider continuing this rhythm for the duration of your small group's discussion of this book, and beyond.

Pray with key Scriptures about God feeding his people. As you read the texts below, prayerfully reflect on your own honest longings and hungers. In a journal, write your own psalm or prayer expressing to God your need for guidance, strength, peace, or whatever you most need right now.

- **John 6.** Read the whole chapter to fill in the context and gaps of the passages discussed today.

- **Exodus 16:19-36**. Reflect on God feeding the Israelites manna.

- **Psalm 63**. Let the phrases of this psalm draw you into personal prayer in your own words.

- **Deuteronomy 8:3** and **Matthew 4:4**. Meditate on these words that Jesus quoted to fend off Satan while fasting in the desert.

Read the essay "No Life In You?" in Appendix E. Jesus' words in John 6 are both bold and clear, but they also must be understood in light of the whole of what God has revealed in Christ through Scripture and Tradition. This short essay lays out a few helpful principles of Catholic theology that protect us from making false assumptions or unjustified conclusions.

Session 3:
From Heaven to Earth

Behold, God's dwelling is
with the human race.
– Revelation 21:3 (NABRE)

Opening Prayer

Invite someone to read the opening prayer.

In the name of the Father, and of the Son, and of the Holy Spirit. Amen.

Heavenly Father, thank you for our group which you have called together to reflect on the indescribable gift of the Eucharist. We gather in your name and trust that you are present here, just as you promised. Guide our hearts, minds, prayers, and discussions today. Give us the grace to long more intently for your presence in our lives, to ponder your precious promises, to learn from your Word and one another, and to grow in faith, hope, and love.

Let us pray:

> *Devoutly I adore You, hidden Deity*
> *Under these appearances concealed.*
> *To You my heart surrenders self*
> *For, seeing You, all else must yield.*

> *Sight and touch and taste here fail;*
> *Hearing only can be believed.*
> *I trust what God's own Son has said.*
> *Truth from truth is best received. [...]*

> *I see no wounds, as Thomas did,*
> *But I profess You God above.*

Draw me deeply into faith,
Into Your hope, into Your love.[1]

Amen.

Opening Discussion

Answer some or all of the following questions

1. Share a high and a low from your life this week.

2. What spoke to you from your prayer this week?

3. In what times or situations do you feel especially close to God, perhaps in nature, at prayer, or with family, etc?

---

1   Thomas Aquinas, "Devoutly I Adore You, Hidden Diety," in *The Aquinas Prayer Book: The Prayers and Hymns of St. Thomas Aquinas*, trans. and ed. By Robert Anderson and Johann Moser (Manchester, NH: Sophia Institute Press, 2000), 69, 71.

Scripture & Tradition

Invite two or three people to read the introductory paragraph and Scripture passage aloud.

Throughout the Scriptures, we see that God persistently desires to be with his people: from the garden, on the way through the desert, in the Temple, and even walking among us as the Incarnate God. Jesus bears the title "Emmanuel" meaning "God with us." How amazing that we have a God that was not content to reign only in heaven but who lowered himself to us, coming to earth in the person of Jesus and giving us the Eucharist so we could touch, see, and hear him in a way we could receive! Today, consider how God continues to draw near to us, particularly through his presence in the Eucharist.

Luke 24:13-35

[13] Now on that same day two of them were going to a village called Emmaus, about seven miles from Jerusalem, [14] and talking with each other about all these things that had happened. [15] While they were talking and discussing, Jesus himself came near and went with them,

[16] but their eyes were kept from recognizing him. [17] And he said to them, "What are you discussing with each other while you walk along?" They stood still, looking sad. [18] Then one of them, whose name was Cleopas, answered him, "Are you the only stranger in Jerusalem who does not know the things that have taken place there in these days?" [19] He asked them, "What things?" They replied, "The things about Jesus of Nazareth, who was a prophet mighty in deed and word before God and all the people, [20] and how our chief priests and leaders handed him over to be condemned to death and crucified him. [21] But we had hoped that he was the one to redeem Israel. Yes, and besides all this, it is now the third day since these things took place. [22] Moreover, some women of our group astounded us. They were at the tomb early this morning, [23] and when they did not find his body there, they came back and told us that they had indeed seen a vision of angels who said that he was alive. [24] Some of those who were with us went to the tomb and found it just as the

women had said; but they did not see him." [25] Then he said to them, "Oh, how foolish you are, and how slow of heart to believe all that the prophets have declared! [26] Was it not necessary that the Messiah should suffer these things and then enter into his glory?" [27] Then beginning with Moses and all the prophets, he interpreted to them the things about himself in all the scriptures.

[28] As they came near the village to which they were going, he walked ahead as if he were going on. [29] But they urged him strongly, saying, "Stay with us, because it is almost evening and the day is now nearly over." So he went in to stay with them. [30] When he was at the table with them, he took bread, blessed and broke it, and gave it to them. [31] Then their eyes were opened, and they recognized him; and he vanished from their sight. [32] They said to each other, "Were not our hearts burning within us while he was talking to us on the road, while he was opening the scriptures to us?" [33] That same hour they got up and returned to Jeru-

salem; and they found the eleven and their companions gathered together. [34] They were saying, "The Lord has risen indeed, and he has appeared to Simon!" [35] Then they told what had happened on the road, and how he had been made known to them in the breaking of the bread.

Discuss

1. When does this encounter take place?

2. How would you describe the disciples' mood or attitude? How can you tell?

3. Do you think these disciples believed the report from the women that Jesus was alive? Why or why not?

4. What were these disciples hoping that Jesus would do and be? How is that the same or different from Jesus' actual mission?

5. Why do you think the disciples urged the veiled Jesus to stay with them (v. 29)?

6. What finally clues in these disciples that they have been talking with Jesus?

7. When did you realize only in hindsight that God had been at work in your life? What made you notice God's presence?

8. How are these disciples changed by the end of the passage? How can you tell?

9. What connections do you see between this passage and the celebration of Mass?

Invite someone to read the following aloud.

St. John Paul II

The Church draws her life from the Eucharist. This truth does not simply express a daily experience of faith, but recapitulates *the heart of the mystery of the Church*. In a variety of ways she joyfully experiences the constant fulfillment of the promise: "Lo, I am with you always, to the close of the age" (Mt 28:20), but in the Holy Eucharist, through the changing of bread and wine into the body and blood of the Lord, she rejoices in this presence with unique intensity. [...]

To contemplate Christ involves being able to recognize him wherever he manifests himself, in his many forms of presence, but above all in the living sacrament of his body and his blood. *The Church draws her life from Christ in the Eucharist;* by him she is fed and by him she is enlightened. The Eucharist is both a mystery of faith and a "mystery of light". Whenever the Church celebrates the Eucharist, the faithful can in some way relive the experience of the two disciples on the road to Emmaus: "their eyes were opened and they recognized him" (Lk 24:31).[2]

Discuss

1. How do you understand God as especially present in the Eucharist? How do you think our discovery of his presence in the Eucharist relates to finding him elsewhere?

2. How has your faith and relationship with Christ "opened your eyes" to a new way

---

2   John Paul II, *Ecclesia de eucharistia* (Vatican City: Vatican Press, 2003), 1, 6.

of understanding your life with its joys and struggles?

3. St. John Paul II talks about the Church drawing her life from the Eucharist. How do you understand this statement?

Final Thoughts

Invite one or two people to read aloud.

Where is God? How close does God get to us?

On the one hand, we affirm that God is everywhere. God is pure spirit, unchanging, existing from all eternity, and therefore is not bound to one or another place or time. God simply *is*.

On the other hand, this same God entered time and space in a particular and decisive way. Though we can never fully understand the mystery of the Incarnation, we affirm that the Almighty and Eternal God took on flesh and came to earth as a man—even as a poor, helpless baby! Even before his death and resurrection, then, this "becoming human" of God meant something wonderful for all humans: "For by his Incarnation the Son of God has united himself in some fashion with every man."[3]

God didn't stop there. The resurrected Word-Made-Flesh became *food*. The eternal God continues even now to bend himself to us in a way we can reach. Jesus veils his splendorous glory and awaits us in every tabernacle around the globe in the humble form of what looks, feels, and tastes like bread and wine but is his Divine Presence. His Body mingles with ours. His Blood runs in our veins. Divine proximity: God is closer than we could ever imagine.

In the week ahead concentrate on drawing close to God even as he draws close to you. Go to Eucharistic adoration or pray before a tabernacle, pray with key Scriptures about the Incarnation, and grow in vulnerability before God.

Bookmark the "Encounter Christ This Week" section on page 43 for help and inspiration for applying today's discussion in your life.

---

3   Paul VI, "Pastoral Constitution on the Church in the Modern
    World, *Gaudium et spes*," in *The Sixteen Documents of Vatican II*, ed.
    by Marianne Lorraine Trouve', FSP (Boston, MA: Pauline Books &
    Media, 1999), 22.

Closing Prayer

Invite someone to lead the group in prayer.

In the name of the Father, and of the Son, and of the Holy Spirit. Amen.

Lord Jesus, Word-made-Flesh and our True Food and Drink, we thank you for spanning the distance for us, for entering the beautiful mess of our world and our very hearts to draw us close to you. We are not worthy of such a gift, and yet, by your own choosing and power, you make us so. Give us grace in the coming week to carve out time for intimate connection with you, for adoration, for Mass, and for loving service to those we encounter.

(Add your own prayers and invite others to pray as well. Close by reciting the following Act of Spiritual Communion prayer together.)

> *My Jesus,*
> *I believe that You are present in the Most Holy*
>   *Sacrament.*
> *I love You above all things,*
> *and I desire to receive You into my soul.*
> *Since I cannot at this moment receive You*
>   *sacramentally,*
> *come at least spiritually into my heart.*
> *I embrace You as if You were already there*

and unite myself wholly to You.
Never permit me to be separated from You.

Amen.

Encounter Christ This Week

Refer to the following pages throughout the week
to incorporate this week's discussion into your life.

Go to Eucharistic adoration or pray before a tabernacle. The mystery of the Real Presence of Christ in the Eucharist is so profound that we need more than explanations, thoughts, and words to fully embrace it. We need regular doses of contemplative silence and solitude in which we simply let God love us and speak the truth into the depths of our souls. There is perhaps no better place to do this than in Eucharistic adoration, where the Blessed Sacrament (the Eucharistic host) is exposed for us to gaze upon silently and peacefully. Of this type of prayer, holy people have said, "I look at him, and he looks at me."[4] This week, carve out at least a half hour for Eucharistic adoration at a nearby Church. If adoration is not available, stop into a Catholic church and sit or kneel in front of the tabernacle in silence and stillness.

---

4   See *Catechism of the Catholic Church*, 2715.

Pray with key Scriptures about the Incarnation. This week, pray with these passages that announce and wonder at the Incarnation of God in Jesus.

- **John 1:1-18.** While the other gospels begin with the birth or baptism of Jesus, St. John's Gospel begins, as the Bible does, "In the beginning." Reflect on the grand perspective John gives right away about who it is that has come in the flesh.

- **Matthew 1:18-25.** St. Matthew tells of the birth of Jesus. Reflect on the meaning of each name used for the Lord in this passage.

- **Philippians 2:1-11.** St. Paul writes of the humble, self-emptying path of downward mobility Christ took in coming to reach and save us. Pray about what this means for you and respond to God in prayer.

- **1 John 1:1-4.** St. John proclaims the eyewitness testimony of the apostles, that "the word of life" has been revealed. How is Jesus a "word of life" to you this week?

- **John 14:1-14.** Reflect on the closeness of the relationship Jesus speaks of here, which not only includes himself and the Father, but all who believe in him.

Let God see you. As we consider how close Jesus draws to us, we discover the call and the privilege of experiencing intimacy with God himself. A helpful way to understand "intimacy" is to think of the phrase, *"into me, see."* This week, try to grow in a habit of radical, courageous intimacy with God who loves you more than you could ever imagine. Don't hide from God behind excessive busyness, or by pretending you're not hurt by someone who mistreated you, or by refusing to examine or acknowledge your sin, or by an unwillingness to ask God or others for help you need. God already knows you better than you know yourself. Come into a more perceptive awareness of your emotions, fears, and joys this week as you abide in some extended times of "into-me-see" with God.

Session 4:
From Time to Eternity

This is the day that the Lord has made;
let us rejoice and be glad in it.
– Psalm 118:24

Opening Prayer

Invite someone to read the opening prayer.

In the name of the Father, and of the Son, and of the Holy Spirit. Amen.

Come, Holy Spirit; breathe your life into us today as we gather here, and guide our conversation. Help us continually to discover our joy, our life, and our hope in you.

Let us pray:

> *Sweetest Jesus,*
> *Body and Blood most holy,*
> *be the delight and pleasure of my soul,*
> *my strength and salvation,*
> *in all temptations,*
> *my joy and peace*
> *in every trial,*
> *my light and guide*
> *in every word and deed,*
> *and my final protection in death.*[1]
Amen.

---

1   Thomas Aquinas, "Short Prayer after Communion," in *The Aquinas Prayer Book: The Prayers and Hymns of St. Thomas Aquinas,* trans. and ed. By Robert Anderson and Johann Moser (Manchester, NH: Sophia Institute Press, 2000), 79.

Opening Discussion

Answer some or all of the following questions.

1. Share a high and a low from your life this week.

2. What spoke to you from your prayer this week?

3. How did your family treat Sundays when you were growing up?

Scripture & Tradition

Invite two or three people to read the introductory paragraph and Scripture passage aloud.

Throughout the Bible, it is clear that God intends for human life to follow a sacred rhythm of work, rest, and worship. "The Lord has blessed the sabbath day and made it holy" (Exodus 20:11, [NABRE]). Holy means "set apart" for God. On the sabbath day, once a week, the people were to observe a "solemn rest" from labor (Exodus 16:23), that they might honor God, be refreshed, and rely on God's provisions. In doing this, the people were called, in a sense, to step *outside* of regular time with all its business, and into God's time, catching a glimpse of eternity.

Since the earliest days, people of faith have observed the sabbath to varying degrees of intensity. Some, like the Israelites in the desert, were slow to heed the Lord's words (see Exodus 16). Others, like some of the Pharisees of Jesus' day, were known for extremely strict observance, labeling more activities as "work" than justified.

As Christians, we believe that the world-changing event of Christ's death and Resurrection brought with it a new and deeper understanding of God's intentions, for which the sabbath tradition was only a foretaste. Read and discuss today how the Christian understanding of the Lord's Day (Sunday) fulfills and replaces the traditional sabbath practice (Saturday), while continuing to root us in the holy rhythm God intends for our good.

Matthew 12:9-14

[9] [Jesus] left that place and entered their synagogue; [10] a man was there with a withered hand, and they asked him, "Is it lawful to cure on the sabbath?" so

that they might accuse him. [11] He said to them, "Suppose one of you has only one sheep and it falls into a pit on the sabbath; will you not lay hold of it and lift it out? [12] How much more valuable is a human being than a sheep! So it is lawful to do good on the sabbath." [13] Then he said to the man, "Stretch out your hand." He stretched it out, and it was restored, as sound as the other. [14] But the Pharisees went out and conspired against him, how to destroy him.

Discuss

1. Some people took the command of sabbath rest so far that they would forbid helping others in need, and Jesus set them straight. What lesson(s) do you think God originally intended for his people by setting one day apart from the rest of the week?

2. Do you generally find it easy or difficult to rest from work / activity? Why do you think that is?

3. What are some different practices or approaches to "keeping holy the sabbath" that you have seen?

Invite someone to read the following aloud.

Catechism of the Catholic Church

1166 "By a tradition handed down from the apostles which took its origin from the very day of Christ's Resurrection, the Church celebrates the Paschal mystery every seventh day, which day is appropriately called the Lord's Day or Sunday."[36] The day of Christ's Resurrection is both the first day of the week, the memorial of the first day of creation, and the "eighth day," on which Christ after his "rest" on the great sabbath inaugurates the "day that the Lord has made," the "day that knows no evening."[37] The Lord's Supper is its center, for there the whole community of the faithful encounters the risen Lord who invites them to his banquet:[38]

> The Lord's day, the day of Resurrection, the day of Christians, is our day. It is called the Lord's day because on it the Lord rose victorious to the Father. If pagans call it the "day of the sun," we

willingly agree, for today the light of the world is raised, today is revealed the sun of justice with healing in his rays.[39]

A day of grace and rest from work

2184 Just as God "rested on the seventh day from all his work which he had done,"[121] human life has a rhythm of work and rest. The institution of the Lord's Day helps everyone enjoy adequate rest and leisure to cultivate their familial, cultural, social, and religious lives.[122]

2185 On Sundays and other holy days of obligation, the faithful are to refrain from engaging in work or activities that hinder the worship owed to God, the joy proper to the Lord's Day, the performance of the works of mercy, and the appropriate relaxation of mind and body.[123] Family needs or important social service can legitimately excuse from the obligation of Sunday rest. The faithful should see to it that legitimate excuses do not lead to habits prejudicial to religion, family life, and health.

> The charity of truth seeks holy leisure—the necessity of charity accepts just work.[124]

2186 Those Christians who have leisure should be mindful of their brethren who have the same needs and the same rights, yet cannot rest from work because of poverty and misery. Sunday is traditionally consecrated by Christian piety to good works and humble service of the sick, the infirm, and the elderly. Christians will also sanctify Sunday by devoting time and care to their families and relatives, often difficult to do on other days of the week. Sunday is a time for reflection, silence, cultivation of the mind, and meditation which furthers the growth of the Christian interior life.[2]

---

2   *Catechism of the Catholic Church*, 1166, 2184-2186. Footnotes from CCC:
36 SC 106
37 Byzantine liturgy.
38 Cf. Jn 21:12; Lk 24:30.
39 St. Jerome, Pasch.: CCL 78,550.
121 Gen 2:2.

Discuss

1. Can you summarize what is meant by the "eighth day"?

2. Is there anything in paragraph 1166 that is particularly new or interesting to you?

3. Reflect on the phrase, "The Lord's Supper is its center" (1166). Do you find it easy or difficult to prioritize Mass on the weekend? How so?

4. "The institution of the Lord's Day helps everyone enjoy adequate rest and leisure to cultivate their familial, cultural, social, and religious lives" (2184). What kinds of activities most refresh you in one or more of these dimensions of life?

5. What instructions or explanations in paragraphs 2184-2186 do you find most helpful? Most affirming? Most challenging?

---

122 Cf. GS 67 § 3.
123 Cf. CIC, can. 120.
124 St. Augustine, De civ. Dei 19,19:PL 41,647.

Final Thoughts

Invite one or two people to read aloud.

It is hard to overstate how strongly the Scriptures and the Church speak about the importance of making the Lord's Day special, holy, set apart from other days. Whether in ancient times or modern-day, both the Jewish sabbath tradition and the Christian meaning of Sunday remind us that God desires his people both to rest and to gather for worship on a weekly basis. This holy rhythm that reminds us of eternity is key to our ongoing transformation and the transformation of the world.

The Church gives us considerable freedom to discern how best to rest from unnecessary labor and cultivate holy leisure according to our varied lives and personalities. The form of our worship on the Lord's Day, however, is not something we determine for ourselves. We are summoned by the Lord himself to gather as a community of faith at the very banquet of his Body and Blood, as he told us: "do this in memory of me" (Luke 22:19).

In the week ahead, enter into the sacredness of Sunday by taking a closer look at your Lord's Day practices, praying with key Scriptures about the Sabbath, and practicing stillness and silence.

Bookmark the "Encounter Christ This Week" section on page 58 for help and inspiration for applying today's discussion in your life.

Closing Prayer

Invite someone to lead the group in prayer.

In the name of the Father, and of the Son, and of the Holy Spirit. Amen.

Father, you teach us the rhythm of work and rest that is good for our bodies, our minds, our families, and our relationship with you. Thank you for caring for our deepest needs and calling us to rest and worship. Help us to live in the light of the New Day that you have created through the Resurrection of our Lord, Jesus Christ.

(Add your own prayers and invite others to pray as well.)

Let us pray:

> *Open wide in joy and love, O Lord, the hearts of these your servants, who have been refreshed with food and drink from on high,*

> *that their home may be a place of decency*
> *and peace and welcome everyone with love.*
> *Through Christ our Lord.*[3]

Amen.

Encounter Christ This Week

Refer to the following pages throughout the week to incorporate this week's discussion into your life.

Take a closer look at your practices of leisure and worship on the Lord's Day. The *Catechism* talks about a variety of ways to set Sunday apart from other days. What are some practices of holy leisure and prayer you'd like to take up? Perhaps a special meal with family, a visit to elderly relatives, taking time in nature, etc? Are there activities or habits that are detracting from your worship or rest? What do you need to stop doing or adjust? Keep in mind that "the Lord's Supper is its center."[4] We all know the difference between trying to squeeze something into our calendars versus building the day around an event. Are there any changes you would need to make to build your Sunday around the celebration of Mass?

---

3   "Prayer After Communion, On Any Anniversary," 1105.
4   *Catechism of the Catholic Church*, 1166.

Pray with key Scriptures about the sabbath and the Lord's Day. Pray with these passages concerning the Jewish sabbath as well as the celebration of the Lord's Day by the early Church.

- **Genesis 1:1-2:4.** God creates the world and rests on the seventh day. Reflect on how the practice of holy rest and leisure makes you more like God himself.

- **Exodus 16:16-36.** This passage, about the manna in the desert, was also assigned after session 2. As you read it this time, reflect especially on the sabbath component of the story. What lesson was God teaching the people by causing the manna to expire when it did? What similarities do you share with the Israelites in their struggle to obey God's ways?

- **Luke 23:50-24:12.** The women anoint Jesus, lay him in the tomb, and return to find him raised on "the first day of the week." Reflect further on the meaning of Sunday as both the *first day* (of the week) and the *eight day* (the Lord's eternal day). What insight does this passage give you about Mass? About life as a disciple?

- **Acts 2:41-47.** The early Christians gather to break bread and praise God. How do you see the actions here reflected in the Mass? Where else are these present in your life outside of Mass?

- **1 Corinthians 11:17-34.** Paul corrects the Corinthians who have lost sight of how to worthily celebrate the Lord's Supper. As you reflect on Paul's words to them, what message do you hear addressed to you today? Allow God's Word to speak to your heart.

Practice silence and stillness. In a world that prizes productivity, action, and busyness, stopping to rest and restore can be difficult for many of us. Get more comfortable with silence and stillness and make space to encounter God not only on Sundays but every day of this week. To do this: find a quiet place, sit on the floor or in an upright chair, and set a timer for however long you want to practice silence and stillness (start with two to five minutes and work up from there.) Take a few deep breaths and invite God to be with you by praying a short prayer like, "Come, Holy Spirit. Be with me here. Teach me how to rest in you." Close your eyes and breathe deeply. Let thoughts or prayers come and go. You can choose to talk to God about those things or return to interior silence until your timer goes off. You can also get more comfortable with silence at other times. This week, let your thoughts and prayers flow as you drive, walk, or do housework in silence, instead of turning on music or a podcast.

Session 5:
From Human to Divine

You are the Body of Christ,
and individually members of it.
– 1 Corinthians 12:27

Opening Prayer

Invite someone to read the opening prayer.

In the name of the Father, and of the Son, and of the Holy Spirit. Amen.

Heavenly Father, thank you for another chance to gather around your Word for prayer, fellowship, and discussion. We seek you today; enlighten our minds with your truth and enflame our hearts with your love. Help us to grow in becoming truly one with you.

Let us pray:

> *Allow me, I plead,*
> *to receive not only*
> *the sacrament of Your Body and Blood*
> *but also*
> *the reality and power of this sacrament.*

> *O most gentle God,*
> *allow me to receive*
> *the Body of Your only begotten Son,*
> *our Lord Jesus Christ,*
> *Who was born of the Virgin Mary*
> *so that I might be worthy*
> *to be united with His Mystical Body*
> *and counted among His members.*

O most loving Father,
give to me
your beloved Son,
Whom I now intend to receive
in this hidden form
but hope to contemplate
face to face for all eternity,

Who with You lives and reigns
in the unity of the Holy Spirit,
world without end.¹

Amen.

Opening Discussion

Answer some or all of the following questions.

1. Share a high and a low from your life this week.

2. What spoke to you from your prayer this week?

---

1   Thomas Aquinas, "Before Communion," in *The Aquinas Prayer Book: The Prayers and Hymns of St. Thomas Aquinas,* trans. and ed. By Robert Anderson and Johann Moser (Manchester, NH: Sophia Institute Press, 2000), 73, 75, 77.

3. How do you understand the term "Body of Christ" as applied to us, the Church?

Scripture & Tradition

Invite two or three people to read the introductory paragraph the quote from St. Cyril of Jerusalem aloud.

You have contemplated Jesus' life-giving sacrifice, the gift of himself to us as true food, his closeness to us as Incarnate God, and his inauguration of a new eternal Day. Yet even talk of Jesus' victory over death and sin and invitation to new life do not capture all that God offers us. We are invited, in the words of St. Peter, to "become participants in the divine nature" (2 Peter 1:4).

What does it mean not just to be *forgiven by* God or *close to* God or *loved by* God or *imitators of* God but actual *participants in* God's own life? The early Church Fathers beckoned us to marvel at this incredible reality by using almost scandalous-sounding phrases such as: "the Son of God became man so that we might become God"[2] and "if you receive [Christ's

---

2 *Catechism of the Catholic Church*, 460, citing St. Athanasius, *De inc.*, 54, 3: PG25, 192B.

Body and Blood] well, you are yourselves what you receive."[3] In today's session consider how Jesus transforms not only bread and wine but also us, his Church, into members of his own Body.

Cyril of Jerusalem

An excerpt from St. Cyril's instructions to newly baptized Christians in the 4th century

> By his own power on a previous occasion he turned the water into wine at Cana in Galilee; so it is surely credible that he has changed wine into blood. If he performed that wonderful miracle just because he had been invited to a human marriage, we shall certainly be much more willing to admit that he has conferred on the wedding-guests the savouring of his body and blood.
>
> So let us partake with the fullest confidence that it is the body and blood of

---

3   St. Augustine, "Easter Sermon 227," *The Works of St. Augustine: A Translation for the 21st Century*, Part III—Sermons, Volume 6: Sermons 184-299z, trans. with notes by John E. Rotelle, O.S.A. (New Rochelle, NY: New York City Press, 1993), 254.

Christ. For his body has been bestowed on you in the form of bread, and his blood in the form of wine, so that by partaking of Christ's body and blood you may share with him the same body and blood. This is how we become bearers of Christ, since his body and blood spreads throughout our limbs; this is how, in the blessed Peter's words, 'we become partakers of the divine nature' [2 Peter 1:4].[4]

Discuss

1. What stands out to you about this quote from St. Cyril of Jerusalem?

2. What miracles does Christ perform in the celebration of the Eucharist at Mass?

3. We are familiar with thinking of many types of groups as "bodies," for example, in phrases like "student body" or "a legislative body." In this sense, a body is a group of people connected to a certain purpose or organization. But Scripture tells us: "You

---

4   Cyril of Jerusalem, "Sermon 4: The Eucharist," in Edward Yarnold, SJ, *The Awe-Inspiring Rites of Initiation: The Origins of R.C.I.A.*, 2nd ed. (Collegeville, MN: The Liturgical Press, 2006), 86-87.

are the Body *of Christ*" (1 Corinthians 12:27, emphasis added). How is being the body *of Christ himself* different from a group of people with a common goal?

4. "For the Son of God became man so that we might become God."[5] What do you think he meant that we "become God"? Why do you think he (and other saints) used such bold and provocative language?

5. Is there a quality or habit you have that you doubt Jesus can really transform? What hope or confidence can you take from St. Cyril's words to apply to yourself?

Invite someone to read the following aloud.

John 13:1-17, 20

[1] Now before the festival of the Passover, Jesus knew that his hour had come to depart from this world and go to the Father. Having loved his own who were in the world, he loved them to the end.

---

5   *Catechism of the Catholic Church*, 460, citing St. Athanasius, *De inc.*, 54, 3: PG25, 192B.

² The devil had already put it into the heart of Judas son of Simon Iscariot to betray him. And during supper ³ Jesus, knowing that the Father had given all things into his hands, and that he had come from God and was going to God, ⁴ got up from the table, took off his outer robe, and tied a towel around himself. ⁵ Then he poured water into a basin and began to wash the disciples' feet and to wipe them with the towel that was tied around him. ⁶ He came to Simon Peter, who said to him, "Lord, are you going to wash my feet?" ⁷ Jesus answered, "You do not know now what I am doing, but later you will understand." ⁸ Peter said to him, "You will never wash my feet." Jesus answered, "Unless I wash you, you have no share with me." ⁹ Simon Peter said to him, "Lord, not my feet only but also my hands and my head!" ¹⁰ Jesus said to him, "One who has bathed does not need to wash, except for the feet, but is entirely clean. And you are clean, though not all of you." ¹¹ For he knew who was to betray him; for this reason he said, "Not all of you are clean."

¹² After he had washed their feet, had put on his robe, and had returned to the table, he said to them, "Do you know what I have done to you? ¹³ You call me Teacher and Lord—and you are right, for that is what I am. ¹⁴ So if I, your Lord and Teacher, have washed your feet, you also ought to wash one another's feet. ¹⁵ For I have set you an example, that you also should do as I have done to you. ¹⁶ Very truly, I tell you, servants are not greater than their master, nor are messengers greater than the one who sent them. ¹⁷ If you know these things, you are blessed if you do them. [...] ²⁰ Very truly, I tell you, whoever receives one whom I send receives me; and whoever receives me receives him who sent me."

Discuss

1. What stands out to you about Jesus in this description of his last night with his disciples?

2. How do you understand Peter's reactions to Jesus in verses 6-10? Why does he initially rebuff Jesus for wanting to wash his feet?

3. Have you ever felt astounded or overwhelmed by someone else's kindness toward you? How did you respond?

4. This passage is part of the Gospel of John's account of the Last Supper. In session 1 you talked about how Jesus taught the disciples what his sacrifice on the Cross would mean by giving them his Body and Blood at the Last Supper. What do you think Jesus is teaching his disciples about his sacrifice in this scene?

5. In verse 20 Jesus tells his disciples that people who receive them receive him. What do you think he means by this? How is it possible for others to receive Jesus in and through us?

Final Thoughts

Invite one or two people to read aloud.

Today you reflected on what it means to be called the "Body of Christ." From the early days of the Church, this phrase has carried three distinct but related meanings: (1) the body of Jesus, which was crucified, raised up from the dead, and ascended to

Heaven; (2) the consecrated Eucharistic host; and (3) the followers of Jesus who receive and participate in the life he offers.

Jesus offers us nothing less than transformation into *himself*! When we consume his Body and Blood with receptive hearts, seeking him first in our lives, we share in his own divine life. We become what we eat.

Consider a weighty implication: some people will not discover the riches of Christ *in the Church* unless and until they first encounter Christ *outside* of Mass, *outside* the parish. How can this occur? Precisely because the Body of Christ leaves the church building and goes into all the nooks and crannies of the world—through us! As we become what we eat, we bear the awesome responsibility, like Mary, of being God-bearers to the world.

This week, reflect on your ongoing transformation into the Body of Christ and how you are called to be Christ for others. Bring a specific intention to place (spiritually) on the altar at Mass, pray with key passages from St. Paul's letters to the Corinthians, and choose a one way to live more like Jesus by reflecting on the spiritual and corporal works of mercy.

Bookmark the "Encounter Christ This Week" section on page 75 for help and inspiration for applying today's discussion in your life.

Closing Prayer

Invite someone to lead the group in prayer.

In the name of the Father, and of the Son, and of the Holy Spirit. Amen.

Lord Jesus, we stand in awe of you. Not only did you cross every distance to draw close to us, but you offer us promises and callings so great we can hardly even begin to understand them. Help us to know what St. Paul called "the love of Christ that surpasses knowledge, so that [we] may be filled with all the fullness of God" (Ephesians 3:19).

(Add your own prayers and invite others to pray as well. Close with this prayer from the Mass below.)

Let us pray:

> *We entreat your majesty most humbly, O Lord, that, as you feed us with the nourishment which comes from the most holy Body and Blood of your Son, so you may make us*

*sharers of his divine nature. Who lives and
reigns for ever and ever.*[6]

Amen.

Encounter Christ This Week

*Refer to the following pages throughout the week to
incorporate this week's discussion into your life.*

What are you bringing to the altar for transformation? At every Mass, we're offered a gloriously unequal gift exchange. We see it most clearly in what happens to the bread and wine: we bring simple gifts of wheat and grapes, "fruit of the earth and the work of human hands," and we receive in return the Body, Blood, Soul, and Divinity of Jesus. A similar dynamic plays out spiritually in our lives. The next time you go to Mass, when the gifts are brought forward to the altar, pray about this question: what are *you* bringing to the altar today? What struggle, hope, fear, joy, boredom, circumstance, regret, etc. are you bringing with you to Mass? Place it on the altar to take part in the glorious exchange. Offer and entrust

---

6   "Prayer After Communion, 28th Sunday in Ordinary Time," 342.

it to Jesus: *"Jesus, I give you* _____ *today. I trust you. Open my heart to receive your life and your love today."*

Pray with a key Scripture about the Body of Christ. Consider St. Paul's description of the Church as the Body of Christ in 1 Corinthians 12:12-27. Pray with the passage and journal about the following questions during one or two prayer times this week.

- As a unique and valued member of the Body of Christ, what are some of your gifts and strengths you're most aware of? How do these gifts allow you to reflect Jesus to others?

- What fears, worries, or actions of yours stem from forgetting or doubting your true identity as a beloved child of God?

- Are you ever tempted to be jealous of the gifts given to other members of the Body? If so, what beliefs or fears might be behind this temptation? Pray for the grace to avoid the discouraging comparison trap and praise God for making you the way you are.

- In the life of grace, even our weaknesses are redeemed and used for good when we cling to Christ. Read and reflect on this amazing fact by opening your Bible to 2 Corinthians 12:1-9, where Paul tells about the "thorn in his flesh" that the Lord would not remove. Write in a journal about whatever lessons lie here for you, in your own pain and weakness.

Choose a way to live more like Jesus. The spiritual and corporal works of mercy are two traditional lists of prayer and action that guide us into living more like Jesus. They also call us to remember that we are united as one body to others who may be suffering or in need of something we can provide. Think creatively: how could you incorporate one or more of these into your life this week?

Corporal Works of Mercy	Spiritual Works of Mercy
Feed the Hungry	Counsel the Doubtful
Give Drink to the Thirsty	Instruct the Ignorant
Shelter the Homeless	Admonish the Sinner
Visit the Sick	Comfort the Sorrowful
Visit the Imprisoned	Forgive Injuries
Bury the Dead	Pray for the Living and the Dead
Give Alms to the Poor	Bear Wrongs Patiently

Session 6:
From the Table
to the World

As the Father has sent me, so I send you.
– John 20:21

Opening Prayer

Invite someone to read the opening prayer.

In the name of the Father, and of the Son, and of the Holy Spirit. Amen.

Jesus, you are the Way, the Truth, and the Life. You go with us always and lead us along the path of everlasting life. Be our guide today, Lord. Come and dwell among us as we discuss your Word, and continue to show us how to be your disciples.

Let us pray:

> *Go before us with heavenly light, O Lord, always and everywhere, that we may perceive with clear sight and revere with true affection the mystery in which you have willed us to participate. Through Christ our Lord.*[1]

Amen.

---

1   "Prayer After Communion, Epiphany," 51.

Opening Discussion

Answer some or all of the following questions.

1. Share a high and a low from your life this week.

2. What spoke to you from your prayer this week?

3. Have you ever felt called to do something that felt outside of your comfort zone? How did you respond?

Scripture and Tradition

Invite two or three people to read the introductory paragraph and Scripture passage aloud.

We don't just leave Mass. We are *sent* back into the world with a job to do. The final command of Jesus on earth and the final act of every Mass is to *go*. "Go therefore and make disciples of all nations" (Matthew 28:19). "Go and announce the Gospel of the Lord."[2] "Go in peace, glorifying the Lord by your life."[3] Faithfully attending Mass is not enough. We

---

2 "The Concluding Rites," 525.
3 *Ibid.*

can't just keep to our families, our Catholic friends, and our parishes. We must *go*.

As the Father sent Jesus, so Jesus sends us (cf. John 20:21). He runs toward the weak; so, therefore, must we. He looks with compassion on the sinner; so, therefore, must we. He sees and loves beyond the divisions in society; so, therefore, must we. He feeds the hungry, visits the sick and imprisoned, comforts the sorrowful, forgives generously, and challenges the status quo. So, therefore, must we. Not perfectly, nor by our own strength; for *his* divine life works *through us* even as it works *on us*. God has always been in the business of writing straight with crooked lines like us.

We can't forget this intrinsic connection between Eucharist and mission. Jesus lives to point everyone to the Father, whose love is better than life and stronger than death; and so, therefore, must we. Transformed people who consume the transformed Body and Blood go forth to transform the world.

Today, reflect on how the Eucharist empowers you to participate in Jesus' mission for the life of the world.

Matthew 28:16-20

[16] Now the eleven disciples went to Galilee, to the mountain to which Jesus had directed them. [17] When they saw him, they worshiped him; but some doubted. [18] And Jesus came and said to them, "All authority in heaven and on earth has been given to me. [19] Go therefore and make disciples of all nations, baptizing them in the name of the Father and of the Son and of the Holy Spirit, [20] and teaching them to obey everything that I have commanded you. And remember, I am with you always, to the end of the age."

Discuss

1. What do you think was going through the disciples' minds as they received the "Great Commission" to go and make disciples of all nations?

2. This commission is issued to all disciples of Jesus. What fears, doubts, or excitement well up when you think about sharing the gospel and making disciples in your life?

3. What promise does Jesus make to his followers? How have you experienced God fulfilling this promise?

4. The disciples were just regular people. How has Jesus prepared them for the mission ahead?

Invite someone to read the following aloud.

Pope Benedict XVI

"The bread I will give is my flesh, for the life of the world" (Jn 6:51). In these words the Lord reveals the true meaning of the gift of his life for all people. These words also reveal his deep compassion for every man and woman. The Gospels frequently speak of Jesus' feelings towards others, especially the suffering and sinners (cf. Mt 20:34; Mk 6:34; Lk 19:41). Through a profoundly human sensibility he expresses God's saving will for all people – that they may have true life. Each celebration of the Eucharist makes sacramentally present the gift that the crucified Lord made of his life, for us and for the whole world. In the Eucharist Jesus also makes us witnesses of God's compassion towards all our brothers and sisters. The eucharistic mystery thus gives rise to a service of charity towards neighbour, which "consists in the very fact that, in God and with God, I love even the person whom I do not like or even know. This can only take place on the basis of an intimate encounter with God, an encounter which has become a communion of will, affecting even my feelings. Then I learn to look on this other person not simply with my eyes and my feelings, but from the perspective of Jesus Christ." (240) In all those I meet, I recognize brothers or sisters for whom the Lord gave his life, loving them "to the end" (Jn 13:1). Our communities, when they celebrate the Eucharist, must become ever more conscious that the sacrifice of Christ is for all, and that the Eucharist thus compels all who believe in him to become "bread that is broken" for others, and to work for the building of a more just and fraternal world. Keeping in mind the multiplication of the loaves and fishes, we need to realize that Christ continues today to exhort his disciples to become personally engaged: "You yourselves, give them something to eat" (Mt 14:16). Each of us is truly called, together with Jesus, to be bread broken for the life of the world.[4]

Discuss

1. Pope Benedict wrote that "In the Eucharist Jesus also makes us witnesses of God's compassion towards all our brothers and sisters." What does the word "compassion" mean? What has the Eucharist shown you about God's care and compassion? How can you be a witness to others of these things?

2. How has the Lord led you to grow in compassion, empathy and love for people you otherwise would rather avoid? Or, is there a situation or person for which you currently need more of "the perspective of Jesus Christ"?

---

4   Benedict XVI, *The Sacrament of Charity: Sacramentum Caritatis* (Vatican City: Vatican Press, 2007), 88.

3. What do you think it means for you to "become bread that is broken for others, and to work for the building of a more just and fraternal world"?

Closing Discussion

As you reach the end of your discussions on the transformative power of the Eucharist, think back over the last six weeks and discuss some or all of the following questions.

1. What scripture passage, quote, or something someone in your group said has stuck with you over the last few weeks?

2. Which of the take-home prayers or practices are you going to continue with going forward?

3. How has your experience of or appreciation for the Eucharist changed?

Final Thoughts

Invite two or three people to read aloud.

Over the last six weeks you have contemplated both the gift and the challenge of the Eucharist. As gift, Jesus comes to us in the Blessed Sacrament, meeting us right where we are. As challenge, what we receive is precisely what (and who) we are called to be for the world. Transformation is needed for both. As the bread and wine are transformed into the Body and Blood, so are we who say "yes" to Jesus transformed into his Body, learning to love like him.

As mentioned in session 1, the Eucharist is the "source and summit of the Christian life."[5] The image in this metaphor is one of a mountain, which itself evokes both a sense of gift (awesome beauty) and challenge (wild, dangerous terrain). "Come, let us go up to the mountain of the Lord, to the house of the God of Jacob; that he may teach us his ways and that we may walk in his paths" (Isaiah 2:3, Micah 4:2). Mountains are prevalent and spiritually meaningful in the Bible. From Mount Sinai where God delivered the Law to Moses to Jesus' Sermon on the Mount to Mount Tabor where Peter, James, and John saw the

---

5 *Catechism of the Catholic Church*, 1324, quoting *Lumen gentium*, 11.

glory of the Lord in the Transfiguration (to name just a few examples), God's revelation is often clearest on a mountain. Transformation happens at the summit, where the view from such heights reaches far beyond that of valleys and plains.

Climbing the mountain of the Lord, then, is a fitting image for what we do at Mass. On the Lord's Day, people come from every direction to ascend the mountain that stands above and beyond normal life, duty, and work. Just as climbing a mountain takes some effort and sacrifice, so does getting to Mass. Once there, on top of that mountain, we are transformed by gaining a far-reaching perspective on life and on the One we worship. From that vantage point, we *look back* at all of history and at the previous week of our own lives, and we *look inward* at our hearts, both to give thanks (*eucharistia*) for the gifts received and to repent of our shortcomings. We *look upward* to God and sing his praises, a little closer to the heavenly choirs of angels singing with us. We hear his Word proclaimed and taught, we reaffirm our faith by reciting the Creed, and we entrust our needs and petitions to God. Then we receive the Bread from Heaven, our food to sustain us as we *look ahead* to the coming week. Finally, having been transformed at the summit a little more, we are re-commissioned as missionaries, sent down from the mountain back to the valleys and plains with good work to do there, and good news to share.

From now on, when you go to Mass, imagine it as a journey up and down "the mountain of the Lord." Consciously *look backward, inward, upward,* and *forward* from that privileged viewpoint, which sheds God's light not only on your own life, but on all of history and creation.

Additionally, this week, cultivate a rhythm of giving thanks to God and others, pray with key Scriptures where Jesus commissions his followers, and identify one tangible way to be good news (gospel) to someone else during the week.

Bookmark the "Encounter Christ This Week" section on page 93 for help and inspiration for applying today's discussion in your life.

Closing Prayer

Invite someone to lead the group in prayer.

In the name of the Father, and of the Son, and of the Holy Spirit. Amen.

Jesus, we give you praise and thanks for nourishing us at the table of your Word in our discussions together. We are forever grateful for all that you have done for us, and for your presence with us in the Eucharist. Continue to transform our hearts, our families, our neighborhoods, and our whole world until we can all rejoice together at your eternal table.

(Add your own prayers and invite others to pray as well.)

Let us pray:

> *I give thanks to You,*
> *Holy Lord, Father almighty, everlasting God.*
>
> *Not through any merit of my own,*
> *but only through the goodness of Your mercy,*
> *You have considered me*
> *— a sinner, a useless servant —*
> *worthy to be nourished*
> *with the precious Body and Blood*
> *of Your Son, our Lord Jesus Christ.*
>
> *I pray to You that this Holy Communion*
> *will not condemn me to punishment*
> *but will rather secure my forgiveness.*
>
> *May it be*
> *an armor of faith*
> *and a shield of good will.*

May it remove my vices
and increase in me
charity,
patience,
humility,
obedience,
and all virtues.

May it be a firm defense
against the plots of all my enemies,
seen and unseen.

May it perfectly quiet my passions,
physical and spiritual.

May it be the firmest bond to You,
the one and true God.

May it give me final happiness.

I also pray that You bring me,
a sinner,
to that ineffable banquet where You dwell
with Your Son
and Holy Spirit.

You Who are for Your saints
true light,
complete fulfillment,
eternal joy,

consummate delight,
and perfect happiness.

Through the same Christ our Lord.[6]

Amen.

Encounter Christ This Week

Refer to the following pages throughout the week to incorporate this week's discussion into your life.

Give thanks *(eucharistia)* **to God.** "Eucharist" comes from a Greek word meaning *thanksgiving*. Cultivate deeper gratitude this week by ending each day thanking God for three specific blessings you encountered that day, be they big or very, very small. When you go to Sunday Mass, make a concerted effort to thank God for the blessings of the past week, and commit the following week into his care. Express your gratitude to people in your life more readily as well. Tell your friend, spouse, colleague, etc. something you appreciate about them. Write a thank you

---

6   Thomas Aquinas, "Longer Prayer After Communion," in
     The Aquinas Prayer Book: The Prayers and Hymns of St. Thomas
     Aquinas, trans. and ed. By Robert Anderson and Johann Moser
     (Manchester, NH: Sophia Institute Press, 2000), 81, 83, 85.

note or email to someone who did a kind deed recently. Expressing gratitude begets more gratitude!

Pray with key Scriptures on the call to mission. Each gospel writer records different details of the final words of Jesus on earth. What themes among them are most prevalent and consistent? What unique details or emphasis does each inspired author give us? As you reflect, remember: the words of Jesus and the New Testament apply not only to the apostles of long ago, but to all who count themselves among the followers of Jesus.

- **Matthew 9:35-38**. The crowds are "like sheep without a shepherd." What does it mean for you to be a "laborer" in the plentiful harvest of the Lord?

- **Mark 16:14-20**. Jesus speaks his last words on earth, according to St. Mark's Gospel. What do these words add to St. Matthew's version that you read together as a group?

- **Luke 24:36-53**. This is the ending of Luke's Gospel, which overlaps with the following reading listed from Acts 1. Read these two together.

- **Acts 1:6-11**. St. Luke wrote the book of Acts as a sequel to his Gospel. Here we get more detail about Jesus' words to the apostles just before his Ascension into heaven. What themes does St. Luke emphasize that are not in Matthew and Mark? How do these words speak to you?

- **John 21:15-19.** St. John's gospel concludes with an intimate exchange between Jesus and Peter. Put yourself in the place of Peter here. What do Jesus' words mean when spoken directly to you? How do you respond to Jesus' loving questions and commands?

Choose one specific way to be good news to someone this week. Ask the Lord in prayer to highlight one person he wants to experience his love through you this week. Ask the Lord to give you a greater share of his own heart for this person. Consider prayerfully what you are called to do with or for them. Perhaps it is quite small: like being cheerful around them, a better listener, or extending a helping hand. Lift them up in prayer too, interceding for their spiritual, physical and emotional needs. Revisit this intention each day in prayer, asking yourself and God how you did in loving this person well. Seek his continued grace and guidance in loving like him.

Appendix A:
Small Group Discussion Guidelines

A small group seeks to foster an honest exploration of Jesus Christ with one another. For many, this will be a new experience. You may be wondering what will take place. Will I fit in? Will I even want to come back?

Here are some expectations and values to help participants understand how small groups work as well as what makes them successful and what doesn't. When a group meets for the first time, the facilitator may want to read the following aloud and discuss it to be sure everyone understands small group parameters.

Purpose

Our express purpose for gathering is to explore together what it means to live the gospel of Jesus Christ in and through the Church.

Priority

In order to reap the full fruit of this personal and communal journey, each one of us will make participation in the weekly gatherings a priority.

Participation

We will strive to create an environment in which all are encouraged to share at their comfort level.

Discussion Guidelines

The purpose of our gathering time is to share in "Spirit-filled" discussion. This type of dialogue occurs when the presence of the Holy Spirit is welcomed and encouraged by the nature and tenor of the discussion. To help this happen, we will observe the following guidelines:

- Participants strive always to be respectful, humble, open, and honest in listening and sharing: they don't interrupt, respond abruptly, condemn what another says, or even judge in their hearts.

- Participants share at the level that is comfortable for them personally.

- Silence is a vital part of the experience. Participants are given time to reflect before discussion begins. Keep in mind that a period of comfortable silence often occurs between individuals speaking.

- Participants are enthusiastically encouraged to share while at the same time exercising care to permit others (especially the quieter members) an opportunity to speak. Each participant should aim to maintain a balance: participating without dominating the conversation.

- Participants keep confidential anything personal that may be shared in the group.

- Perhaps most important, participants should cultivate attentiveness to the Holy Spirit's desire to be present in the time spent together. When the conversation seems to need help, ask for the Holy Spirit's intercession silently in your heart. When someone is speaking of something painful or difficult, pray that the Holy Spirit comforts that person. Pray for the Spirit to aid the group in responding sensitively and lovingly. If someone isn't participating, praying for that person during silence may be more helpful than a direct question. These are a few examples of the ways in which each person might personally invoke the Holy Spirit.

Time

It is important that your group start and end on time. Generally, a group meets for about ninety minutes, with an additional thirty minutes or so afterwards for refreshments. Agree on these times as a group, and work to honor them.

Appendix B:
A Guide to Seeking God
in Prayer and Scripture

*Unless you are convinced that prayer is the best
use of your time, you will never find time to pray.*
—*Fr. Hilary Ottensmeyer, OSB*[1]

If only I had the time!

Time—we only have so much of it each day. All kinds
of demands chip away the hours. Modern communication and social media increase our sense of ur-
gency. No wonder we experience conflicting desires
over how to spend our time.

One thing we all know for certain: relationships require time. Friendships don't form or last unless people spend time together. Marriages struggle when

---

1   Br. Francis de Sales Wagner, OSB, ed., *Sacred Rhythms: The Monastic
    Way Every Day* (St. Meinrad, IN: Abbey Press, 2014), 5.

spouses don't make time to talk and listen deeply to one another. Parents who do not prioritize spending time with their children risk painfully regretting that decision down the road. Some things never change. We were made for relationships, and relationships take time.

So how about our relationship with God?

Just as all relationships require time, so too does a deepening friendship with God. What kind of relationship do you have with the person in your neighborhood with whom you've never had a personal conversation? Even if you take out her garbage can weekly because she is disabled, she is an acquaintance, not a friend. Friends spend time together. Jesus called us his friends (John 15:15).

One way we spend time with Jesus is at Mass. This will always be the center, source, and summit of our prayer lives. But without personal time with Jesus outside liturgies, the encounter at Mass can resemble meeting that neighbor at a block party: talking for a few minutes without any deep connection. The mysterious reality of that person remains remote.

How much time should I spend in personal prayer?

A little goes a long way with God. Start small and work up to more. If you're not already in the practice of prioritizing a daily prayer time, start with fifteen minutes if you can. If that proves too difficult, try ten, or even, five minutes.

Prayer begets prayer. As you experience the fruit of a deeper friendship with the Lord, your desire for God grows. Your heart longs more and more to build your life around prayer rather than just squeezing it in. Hunger for God grows when you taste the sweetness of Jesus' company and experience the joy of a Christ-centered life.

Basics of Spending Time with God in Prayer

Always begin by recognizing that God is with you. He is with you even when you're not paying attention. When you attend to God, you are simply focusing on reality.

St. Teresa of Ávila called prayer "an intimate sharing between friends."[2] Any good friendship involves three things: talking, listening, and simply being together.

---

2   Teresa of Ávila, *The Book of Her Life*, trans. by Kieran Kavanaugh, OCD, and Otilio Rodriguez, OCD (Indianapolis, IN: Hackett Publishing Company, 2008), 44.

1. Talk to God

There is no wrong way to talk to God. Talk about anything on your mind. Keep it real; don't just say what you think a prayerful person should say or what you think God wants to hear. Even saying, "Lord, help me to pray" is itself a prayer.

If you're stuck, keep in mind the first three things we all learn to say as children: "Thank you," "I'm sorry," and "Please." That's a great outline for a chat with God—it's as simple as that!

2. Listen to God

Morning after morning / he wakens my ear to hear.
—Isaiah 50:4 (NABRE)

No matter how impossible it may seem, you can learn to discern the Lord's voice in your life. It takes practice and guidance, but never forget this promise of Jesus: "My sheep hear my voice, and I know them, and they follow me" (John 10:27). Jesus means what he says—this is attainable!

The fastest way to learn to recognize the voice of God is to read the Scriptures prayerfully. The Bible truly is God's word expressed in human words. With the Holy Spirit coming to our aid, reading it becomes "a life-giving encounter."[3] On the following pages, a simple outline of *lectio divina* will help you to find out what the Lord wants to say to you through Scripture. *Lectio divina* is a time-tested way of encountering the voice of the living God in Scripture.

3. Be with God

Sometimes words get in the way of deeper communication. St. John of the Cross said, "The Father spoke one Word, which was his Son, and this Word he speaks always in eternal silence, and in silence must it be heard by the soul."[4] The Lord says, "Be still, and know that I am God" (Psalm 46:10).

Begin and end each prayer time with a minute or two of silence to rest in God's presence. You probably won't hear anything audible or even sense anything interiorly, but be confident that God is filling that silence in ways you cannot immediately perceive. Often something can become very clear later in the day after a time of silence in the morning.

---

3   John Paul II, *Novo millennio ineunte,* apostolic letter, Vatican website, January 6, 2001, https://www.vatican.va/content/john-paul-ii/en/apost_letters/2001/documents/hf_jp-ii_apl_20010106_no-vo-millennio-ineunte.html.

4   John of of the Cross, *The Collected Works of St. John of the Cross,* trans. by Kieran Kavanaugh, OCD, and Otilio Rodriguez, OCD (Washington, DC: ICS Publications, 1991), 92.

Lectio Divina: **Putting It All Together**

One of the best ways to "talk," "listen," and "be with" God in a single sitting is the time-honored method of praying with Scripture called *lectio divina* (Latin for "divine reading"). This ancient practice has seen dramatic growth in popularity since Vatican II, partly due to the loud and clear call of every pope since the council for laity and clergy alike to discover (or rediscover) this treasure. For example, Pope Benedict XVI said the following:

> I would like in particular to recall and recommend the ancient tradition of *Lectio divina:* the diligent reading of Sacred Scripture accompanied by prayer brings about that intimate dialogue in which the person reading hears God who is speaking, and in praying, responds to him with trusting openness of heart (cf. *Dei verbum*, 25). If it is effectively promoted, this practice will bring to the Church—I am convinced of it—a new spiritual springtime.[5]

---

5   Benedict XVI, "Address to Participants in the International Congress Organized to Commemorate the 40th Anniversary of *Dei verbum*, September 16, 2005," https://www.vatican.va/content/benedict-xvi/en/speeches/2005/september/documents/hf_ben-xvi_spe_20050916_40-dei-verbum.html.

The term *lectio divina* is often associated with St. Benedict of Nursia of the sixth century. *The Rule of St. Benedict* assigned monks to meditate upon Scripture at specific hours of the day. In the Middle Ages, four steps came to specify the process: *Lectio* (reading), *meditatio* (meditation/reflection), *oratio* (prayer), and *contemplatio* (contemplation or resting in God's presence).

Lectio teaches us to listen intently for a specific word or phrase that stands out, whether boldly or ever so gently. As believers, we trust that the Holy Spirit aids our reading of the Scripture. When something stands out or troubles us in a reading, this is God's personal word for us to think about (meditation) and discuss with Jesus (prayer or *oratio*).

If you find it difficult to remember the four aspects of *lectio divina*, four "Rs" give a simple and memorable description: read, reflect, respond, rest. See more below.

The Four Rs: A Method for *Lectio Divina*

Preparation: Begin with the Sign of the Cross. Take a moment to be quiet and still. Ask the Holy Spirit to guide your time.

1. **Read.** Read the Scripture selection slowly and attentively. Note any word, phrase, or image that catches your attention. It's helpful to read the passage more than once and/or out loud.

2. **Reflect.** Think about the meaning of whatever caught your attention. The Holy Spirit drew you to it for a reason. What line of thought do you pursue in response? Notice any questions that arise or any emotions you experience. Return to the text as often as you wish.

3. **Respond.** Talk to God about the passage, your thoughts, or anything else on your heart. Thank him for the blessings you have received. Ask him for your own needs, as well as the needs of others. Note any changes or actions you want to make. If the Holy Spirit leads you to any resolution or application in your life, writing it down will help you remember. Ask God to help you live it out.

4. **Rest.** Rest a few minutes in silence with the Lord. "Be still, and know that I am God" (Psalm 46:11). This period of rest allows the

meditations and prayers of the day to sink down from your mind to your heart, as you linger in the Father's loving embrace.

Appendix C:
A Guide to the Sacrament of Reconciliation

God gave the Church a visible means of experiencing his reconciling love after baptism. In the Sacrament of Reconciliation, we see, hear, touch, feel, and know, with blessed assurance, that we are embraced, forgiven, healed, and strengthened by the Lord himself. This truly is good news!

This appendix contains an examination of conscience based on the Ten Commandments and a brief guide to the steps in receiving the sacrament.

Examination of Conscience

Use the prompts below to review your actions, thoughts, and attitudes. Make note of sins and omissions to confess, either mentally or written on a piece of paper, to bring with you to confession.

Let your conscience speak to you:

- When have I neglected to do what I knew was good?

- When have I chosen to do what I knew was evil or against God's will?

- When have I thought or acted in a way that was unloving to myself or others?

- When have I neglected to love God?

Examine your conscience in light of the Ten Commandments:

1. I am the Lord your God: you shall not have strange Gods before me.

   - Have I put people, things, or events ahead of God?

   - Have I spent time with God in prayer each day?

2. You shall not take the name of the Lord your God in vain.

   • Have I used my words to defame God, others, or the Church?

3. Remember to keep holy the Lord's Day.

   • Have I attended Mass every Sunday and on other Holy Days?

   • Do I put God ahead of my work and other responsibilities and set aside intentional time to be with God?

4. Honor your father and your mother.

   • Have I shown my parents love and respect?

   • Have I made efforts to communicate with and visit my parents where possible?

   • Am I holding any grudges or resentment over my parents' shortcomings?

5. You shall not kill.

   • Have I physically or emotionally harmed anyone?

- Have I damaged others' reputation through gossip or slander?

- Have I been mean or unjustly angry to others?

6. You shall not commit adultery.

   - Have I respected the sexual dignity due myself and others?

   - Have I lusted after someone physically or emotionally?

   - Have I engaged in illicit romantic fantasies, used pornography, or masturbated?

7. You shall not steal.

   - Have I taken physical or intellectual property that does not belong to me?

   - Have I hoarded, wasted, or otherwise improperly used money or resources?

8. You shall not bear false witness against your neighbor.

   - Have I lied to, misled, or manipulated others?

- Have I stayed quiet when I ought to have defended another?

9. You shall not covet your neighbor's spouse.

- Have I been inappropriately intimate (physically or emotionally) with someone who is not my spouse?

- Have I sought the romantic attention of others through inappropriate flirtation or immodesty?

10. You shall not covet your neighbor's goods.

- Do I seek to outstrip others for the sake of status or power?

- Do I compare myself to others unnecessarily?

- Do I rely on the Lord for my needs?

- Have I harbored envy or jealousy?

Talk to God about the things that examining your conscience stirred up in you. Express your sorrow and contrition to God and resolve to repent and participate in the Sacrament of Reconciliation as soon as possible.

If it has been a long time since you last went to confession—or if you've never been—you may be hesitant and unsure. Don't let these very common feelings get in your way. Reconciling with God and the Church always brings great peace. Take the plunge—you will be glad you did!

If it will help to alleviate your fears, familiarize yourself with the step-by-step description of the process below. Most priests are happy to help anyone willing to take the risk. If you forget anything, the priest will remind you. So don't worry about committing every step and word to memory. Remember, Jesus isn't giving you a test; he just wants you to experience the grace of his mercy!

Catholics believe that the priest acts in *persona Christi*, as the person of Christ. The beauty of the sacraments is that they touch us both physically and spiritually. On the physical level in confession, we hear the words of absolution through the person of the priest. On the spiritual level, we know that it is Christ assuring us that he has truly forgiven us. We are made clean!

You usually have the option of going to confession anonymously—in a confessional booth or in a room with a screen—or face-to-face with the priest. Whatever your preference is fine with the priest.

Steps in the Sacrament of Reconciliation

1. Prepare to receive the sacrament by praying and examining your conscience. If you need help, you can find many different lists of questions online that will help you examine your conscience.

2. Once you're with the priest, begin by making the Sign of the Cross while greeting the priest with these words: "Bless me father, for I have sinned." Then tell him how long it has been since your last confession. If it's your first confession, tell him so.

3. Confess your sins to the priest to the best of your recollection. If you are unsure about anything, ask him to help you. Place your trust in God, who is a merciful and loving Father. When you are finished, indicate this by saying, "I am sorry for these and all of my sins."

4. The priest will assign you a penance, such as a prayer, a Scripture reading, or a work of mercy, service, or sacrifice.

5. Express sorrow for your sins by saying an Act of Contrition, such as the one below. Or you may pray in your own words if desired.

Act of Contrition

My God, I am sorry for my sins with all my heart. In choosing to do wrong, and failing to do good, I have sinned against you whom I should love above all things. I firmly intend, with your help, to do penance, to sin no more, and to avoid whatever leads me to sin. Our Savior Jesus Christ suffered and died for us. In his name, my God, have mercy.

6. The priest, acting in the person of Christ, will absolve you from your sins by saying, "I absolve you from your sins in the name of the Father, and of the Son, and of the Holy Spirit." You respond by making the Sign of the Cross and saying, "Amen."

7. The priest may offer some proclamation of praise.

8. The priest will dismiss you, often with the words "Your sins are forgiven. Go in peace."

9. Be sure to complete your assigned penance as soon as possible.

Appendix D:
Lamb of God

If you've ever attended a Seder meal with a Jewish friend, you may have found this Passover meal eerily familiar. That's because the first celebration of the Eucharist took place at a Passover meal, when Jesus celebrated it with the Twelve Apostles shortly before his death. Jesus used the celebration of Passover to help his followers (and us) understand what his sacrifice on the Cross would mean.

The Jewish celebration of Passover is an annual remembrance of a central event in Jewish and Christian history: God freeing the Israelites from slavery under Pharoah. God and Moses first challenged Pharaoh's rule with words and demonstration of God's power. But when Pharaoh wouldn't budge, a battle ensued, even going so far as God sending a plague of death throughout the land. To protect the Israelites from the angel of death passing through Egypt, God instructed them to slaughter an unblemished lamb and smear its blood across the thresholds of their homes. Death passed over those who offered this sacrifice to God. The Israelites then prepared the lamb along with unleavened bread as a final meal before their journey from slavery into freedom.

In the desert, when they were free of Pharaoh's dominion, God told the Israelites more about his intentions. Not only had he freed them from slavery in Egypt, he freed them for a purpose. He had chosen them as his own people, a nation that would worship him as the one true God, live according to his ways, and witness to him before all the other nations. He would unite them as a people and lead them to the Promised Land. The people agreed saying, "All that the Lord has spoken we will do" (Exodus 24:7). So Moses made an animal sacrifice and sprinkled the blood on the altar before the Lord and on the Israelites saying, "See the blood of the covenant that the Lord has made with you in accordance with all these words" (Exodus 24:8). With the blood of the animal sacrifice Moses solemnly sealed the covenant between God and the people.

This history, very familiar to the Jewish people, is in the background when Jesus gathers his disciples for his Last Supper. He took the bread at the table and said, "This is my body, which is given for you" (Luke 22:19). Then he took the wine saying, "This cup that is poured out for you is the new covenant in my blood" (Luke 22:20). Jesus, the "Lamb of God who takes away the sin of the world," as John the Baptist proclaimed (John 1:29), is teaching us that his sacrifice is the new Passover: he is the unblemished lamb sacrificed to save us from death. He conquers the dominion of sin and leads us from slavery into freedom. He is the mediator of a new covenant with God, sealed in his blood. He establishes us as God's holy people, set apart to worship him, follow in his ways, and witness to him in all the earth. And he gives himself to us as true food so that through his power within us we can remain faithful to God and make it safely through this exile to the final Promised Land of heaven.

Appendix E:
No Life in You?

In John 6, Jesus proclaims bold, shocking, hard-to-understand truths. One of them is this: "Very truly, I tell you, unless you eat the flesh of the Son of Man and drink his blood, you have no life in you" (6:53).

How do we make sense of this? Does this mean that those who do not attend Mass are necessarily spiritually *dead*? Or, alternatively, does it mean that everyone who receives the Eucharist is automatically full of divine life?

To both of these questions, we must answer *no*. When we carefully read this text alongside Catholic Tradition and Magisterium, we can see some important principles at play. First, the Eucharist is not magic. Taking communion is not some ticket to heaven or to guaranteed transformation in Christ. As Jesus himself says several times in this discourse in

John 6, believing in him is what brings us divine life: "This is indeed the will of my Father, that all who see the Son and believe in him may have eternal life; and I will raise them up on the last day" (John 6:40).

St. Paul thus warns against a casual, faithless participation in the Lord's Supper:

> Whoever, therefore, eats the bread or drinks the cup of the Lord in an unworthy manner will be answerable for the body and blood of the Lord. Examine yourselves, and only then eat of the bread and drink of the cup. For all who eat and drink without discerning the body, eat and drink judgment against themselves (1 Corinthians 11:27-29).

While the sacraments unfailingly mediate God's grace to us, we must also *choose* to receive these gifts with faith, conversion of heart, and a growing openness to God's will. In the language of theologians, we must cultivate the proper *interior dispositions* to receive the sacraments fruitfully. The crowds were pressing in on Jesus, but only the woman who touched his garment in earnest faith and dependent need (an earnest interior disposition) was deeply affected by the power he contained (Luke 8:43-48).

Second, while God offers us the incredible gifts of the sacraments, including the Eucharist, as the foundational, normative, ordinary, promised way to receive his grace and live connected to him, God is never bound to work *exclusively* within the sacraments or the visible confines of the Church. The Spirit blows where it wills (cf. John 3:8) and is mysteriously at work in ways we can never perfectly dissect or discern. In several authoritative documents, the Church affirms the distinct possibility of God's grace working in the hearts of those who seek and respond to God in the depths of conscience and through those parts of their traditions that reflect and convey truth.[1]

We approach the Eucharist with faithful expectation because Jesus has *promised* us that we will find life there: "Whoever eats me will live because of me" (John 6:57). Because of this promise and the millennia of lived experience among the faithful, we know that we can depend on the Eucharist as a place of sustenance and encounter with God's life and presence. But we can't limit God's ability to work outside the normative channels of grace.

---

1 See *Lumen gentium*, 16 and *Nostra aetate*, 2, for starters. You can find these documents of the Second Vatican Council at www.vatican.va.

The above principles keep us humble and protect us from getting sidetracked into speculative pondering about who exactly has God's life within them and who does not; or who is "saved" or "not saved"; "in" or "out." We leave such matters to God as we "work out [our] own salvation with fear and trembling" (Philippians 2:12) and joyfully witness to others the reality of Christ's saving love.

Appendix F:
The Role of a Facilitator

Perhaps no skill is more important to the success of a small group than the ability to facilitate a discussion lovingly. It is God's Holy Spirit working through our personal spiritual journey, not necessarily our theological knowledge, that makes this possible.

The following guidelines can help facilitators avoid some of the common pitfalls of small group discussion. The goal is to open the door for the Spirit to take the lead and guide your every response because you are attuned to his movements. Pray daily and especially before your small group meeting. This way you can learn to sense the Spirit's gentle promptings when they come!

You are a Facilitator, Not a Teacher

As a facilitator, it can be extremely tempting to answer every question. You may have excellent answers and be excited about sharing them with your brothers and sisters in Christ. However, a more Socratic method, by which you attempt to draw answers from participants, is much more fruitful for everyone else and for you as well.

Get in the habit of reflecting participants' questions or comments to the whole group before offering your own input. It is not necessary for you as a facilitator to enter immediately into the discussion or to offer a magisterial answer. When others have sufficiently addressed an issue, try to exercise restraint in your comments. Simply affirm what has been said; then thank them and move on.

If you don't know the answer to a question, have a participant look it up in the *Catechism of the Catholic Church* and read it aloud to the group. If you cannot find an answer, ask someone to research the question for the next session. Never feel embarrassed to say, "I don't know." Simply acknowledge the quality of the question and offer to follow up with that person after you do some digging. Remember, you are a facilitator, not a teacher.

Affirm and Encourage

We are more likely to repeat a behavior when it is openly encouraged. If you want more active participation and sharing, give positive affirmation to the responses of the group members. This is especially important if people are sharing from their hearts. A simple "Thank you for sharing that" can go a long way in encouraging further discussion in your small group.

If someone has offered a theologically questionable response, don't be nervous or combative. Wait until others have offered their input. It is very likely that someone will proffer a more helpful response, which you can affirm by saying something such as, "That is the Catholic perspective on that topic. Thank you."

If no acceptable response is given and you know the answer, exercise great care and respect in your comments so as not to appear smug or self-righteous. You might begin with something such as, "Those are all interesting perspectives. What the Church has said about this is . . . "

Avoid Unhelpful Tangents

Nothing can derail a Spirit-filled discussion more quickly than digressing on unnecessary tangents. Try to keep the session on track. If conversation strays from the topic, ask yourself, "Is this a Spirit-guided tangent?" Ask the Holy Spirit too! If not, bring the group back by asking a question that steers conversation to the Scripture passage or to a question you have been discussing. You may even suggest kindly, "Have we gotten a little off topic?" Most participants will respond positively and get back on track through your sensitive leading.

That being said, some tangents may be worth pursuing if you sense a movement of the Spirit. It may be exactly where God wants to steer the discussion. You will find that taking risks can yield some beautiful results.

Don't Fear the Silence

Be okay with silence. Most people need a moment or two to come up with a response to a question. It is quite natural to need some time to formulate our thoughts and put them into words. Some may need a moment just to gather the courage to speak at all.

Regardless of the reason, don't be afraid of a brief moment of silence after asking a question. Let everyone in the group know early on that silence is an integral part of normal small group discussion. They needn't be anxious or uncomfortable when it happens. God works in silence!

This applies to times of prayer as well. If no one shares or prays after a sufficient amount of time, just move on gracefully.

The Power of Hospitality

A little hospitality can go far in creating community. Everybody likes to feel cared for. This is especially true in a small group whose purpose it is to connect to Jesus Christ, a model for care, support, and compassion.

Make a point to greet people personally when they first arrive. Ask them how their day has been going. Take some time to invest in the lives of your small group participants. Pay particular attention to newcomers. Work at remembering each person's name. Help everyone feel comfortable and at home. Allow your small group to be an environment where authentic relationships take shape and blossom.

Encourage Participation

Help everyone to get involved, especially those who are naturally less vocal or outgoing. To encourage participation initially, always invite various group members to read aloud the selected readings. Down the road, even after the majority of the group feels comfortable sharing, you may still have some quieter members who rarely volunteer a response to a question but would be happy to read.

Meteorology?

Keep an eye on the "Holy Spirit barometer." Is the discussion pleasing to the Holy Spirit? Is this conversation leading participants to a deeper personal connection to Jesus Christ? The intellectual aspects of our faith are certainly important to discuss, but conversation can sometimes degenerate into an unedifying showcase of intellect and ego. Other times discussion becomes an opportunity for gossip, detraction, complaining, or even slander. When this happens, you can almost feel the Holy Spirit leaving the room!

If you are aware that this dynamic has taken over a discussion, take a moment to pray quietly in your heart. Ask the Holy Spirit to help you bring the conversation to a more wholesome topic. This can often be achieved simply by moving to the next question.

Pace

Each session in this guide is intended for a 90-minute small group format. While we strongly recommend 90-minute sessions, you may wish to adjust these slightly according to your own group's size, style, and desired length. For example, if you have just three people that meet before work or school, you could theoretically keep each session to 60 or 75 minutes. Whatever you choose, be sure to start and end on time to honor each person's time and other commitments. See the following timing guide to help you navigate each session in this book. They add up to 90 minutes each, including ten minutes of flex time per session.

Session 1 Timing Guide:

- Group Introductions: 10 minutes

- Opening Prayer: 5 minutes

- Opening Discussion: 10 minutes

- Scripture and Tradition: 45 minutes

- Final Thoughts: 5 minutes

- Closing Prayer: 5 minutes

- [Flex Time: 10 minutes]

Sessions 2-5 Timing Guide:

- Opening Prayer: 5 minutes

- Opening Discussion: 10 minutes

- Scripture and Tradition: 50 minutes

- Final Thoughts: 5 minutes

- Closing Prayer: 10 minutes

- [Flex Time: 10 minutes]

Session 6 Timing Guide:

- Opening Prayer: 5 minutes

- Opening Discussion: 10 minutes

- Scripture and Tradition: 40 minutes

- Closing Discussion: 10 minutes

- Final Thoughts: 5 minutes

- Closing Prayer: 10 minutes

- [Flex Time: 10 minutes]

Generally, you want to pace the session to finish in the allotted time, but sometimes this may be impossible without sacrificing quality discussion. If you reach the end of your meeting and find that you have covered only half the material, don't fret! This is often the result of lively Spirit-filled discussion and meaningful theological reflection.

In such a case, you may take time at another meeting to cover the remainder of the material. If you have only a small portion left, you can ask participants to pray through these on their own and come to the following meeting with any questions or insights they might have. Even if you must skip a section to end on time, make sure you leave adequate time for prayer and to review the "Encounter Christ This Week" section. This is vital in helping participants integrate their discoveries from the group into their daily lives.

Genuine Friendships

The best way to show Jesus' love and interest in your small group members is to meet with them for coffee, dessert, or a meal outside of your small group time.

You can begin by suggesting that the whole group get together for ice cream or some other social event outside of your small group time. Socializing will allow relationships to develop by providing the opportunity for different kinds of conversation than what happens during the group.

You will notice an immediate difference in the quality of community in your small group at the next meeting.

After that first group social, try to meet one-on-one with each person in your small group. This allows for more in-depth conversation and personal sharing, giving you the chance to know each participant better so that you can love and care for them as Jesus would.

Jesus called the twelve apostles in order that they could be "with him" (Mark 3:14). When people spend time together, eat together, laugh together, cry together, and talk about what matters to them, an intense Christian community develops. That is the kind of community Jesus was trying to create, and that must be the kind of community we try to create, because it changes lives. And changed lives change the world!

Joy

Remember that seeking the face of the Lord brings joy! Nothing is more fulfilling, more illuminating, and more beautiful than to foster a deep and enduring relationship with Jesus Christ. Embrace your group members and the entire spiritual life with a spirit of joyful anticipation of what God wants to accomplish.

These things I have spoken to you, that my joy may be in you, and that your joy may be full (John 15:11).

Small Group Discussion Guides from the Evangelical Catholic

When people meet the real Jesus in Scripture, lives change, hearts heal, and the grace and power of our Baptism is unleashed to make us "ambassadors for Christ" (2 Corinthians 5:20).

Using the following discussion guides, well-formed and trained leaders who've learned to facilitate dynamic Scripture discussions can be instruments of the Holy Spirit revealing the person of Jesus.

Order books at evangelicalcatholic.org.

Encounter Series

The Evangelical Catholic's Encounter Series of books and resources are designed to connect people with Jesus through prayer and Scripture. They are approachable for anyone desiring a deeper experience of Jesus.

Believe: Meeting Jesus in the Scriptures

The six sessions in *Believe: Meeting Jesus in the Scriptures* focus on episodes when Jesus changed people's lives. Get to know Jesus as he heals a blind man, mourns the death of a friend, and has compassion on the people he meets. The questions that follow spark discussion and allow participants to consider how the story applies to their own lives.

Amazed and Afraid: Discover the Power of Jesus

Dive into the Gospels and begin a regular pattern of prayer. Each of the six sessions in *Amazed and Afraid: Discover the Power of Jesus* features a scene about Jesus and his disciples, followed by a series of questions to help participants reflect more deeply about their relationship with God.

Signs and Wonders: Encountering Jesus of Nazareth

The Gospels show us what Jesus cared about, how he treated people, and what he thought was most important in life. The six sessions of *Signs and Wonders: Encountering Jesus of Nazareth* include some of the most dramatic Gospels episodes: the wedding at Cana, Jesus walking on water, and the raising of the little girl who had died.

Establish Series

The Evangelical Catholic's Establish Series of books and resources help participants build a solid foundation of discipleship in their lives. They are perfect for anyone ready to grow their commitment to following Jesus.

The Way: Becoming a Disciple of Jesus

As Catholic disciples of Jesus, we mature to the extent that we allow the heart and habits of Jesus and his people to become ever more our own. The twelve sessions of *The Way* invite individuals and groups to reflect upon the heart and habits of discipleship with Scripture, discussion questions, and prompts for spiritual exercises.

We reflect on the call to know God as friend, savior, and source of all life through Jesus Christ. Over the course of twelve sessions, we discuss how to nurture this friendship in prayer and in Scripture.

Transformed: The Gift and Challenge of the Eucharist

The Eucharist comes to us both as an indescribable gift and a profound challenge. What effect does this sacred mystery have on us? In a word, *transformation*. As the bread and wine are truly transformed into the Body and Blood of Jesus, we who receive this heavenly meal with open hearts are continually transformed into people who love like Jesus—and loving like Jesus transforms the world.

In this six-week discussion guide for Catholic small groups, participants read and discuss key selections from Scripture, saints, and Church teaching around the transformational power and promise of the Eucharist.

With Jesus to the Cross: Lenten Guides on the Sunday Mass Readings

On the night before he died, Jesus made this promise to his disciples: "If you continue in my word, you are truly my disciples, and you will know the truth, and the truth will make you free" (John 8:31-32). With Jesus to the Cross makes it easy to dive into the Lenten Sunday Mass readings. Gather a small group weekly to discuss them, or consider the thought-provoking questions on your own. Available for liturgical years A, B, and C.

About the Evangelical Catholic

The Evangelical Catholic (EC) is a Catholic non-profit consulting ministry based in Madison, Wisconsin. The Evangelical Catholic delights to partner with Catholic ministry leaders to equip everyday Catholics to live out the great commission.

In 1997, Tim and Sandy Cruse started a small group of Catholics in their home. This group experienced Jesus powerfully through intimate friendship, rich Scripture discussions, and shared sacramental experiences. After one year, the people from this group went out to form their own small groups with friends, co-workers, neighbors, and family that they hoped would come to experience Jesus in the same way. With immense joy, these leaders experienced that they could make disciples by the power of the Holy Spirit given to them in their Baptism.

Filled with the Holy Spirit, these leaders sparked a movement of evangelization that extended to reach more and more people. As word spread about this expanding movement of evangelization, the EC helped other ministries launch lay people into mission by leading training events, writing small group guides, and traveling to ministries across the United States.

Today, the Evangelical Catholic works with hundreds of parishes, campus ministries, and military chaplaincies worldwide. Our prayer is that through the grace of the Holy Spirit, we can help make the Church's mission of evangelization accessible, natural, and fruitful for every Catholic, and that many lives will be healed and transformed by knowing Jesus within the Church.

Learn more at evangelicalcatholic.org.

www.ingramcontent.com/pod-product-compliance
Lightning Source LLC
Chambersburg PA
CBHW060528130626
46553CB00002B/688

* 9 7 9 8 9 8 9 1 3 6 6 2 9 *